Midnight Lantern

Books by Tess Gallagher

POETRY

Dear Ghosts,
My Black Horse: New and Selected Poems
Portable Kisses
Moon Crossing Bridge
Amplitude: New and Selected Poems
Willingly
Under Stars
Instructions to the Double

FICTION

The Man from Kinvara: Selected Stories
Barnacle Soup: Stories from the West of Ireland (with Josie Gray)
At the Owl Woman Saloon
The Lover of Horses and Other Stories

ESSAYS

Beyond Forgetting: Poetry and Prose about Alzheimer's Disease
(edited by Holly J. Hughes, introduction by Tess Gallagher)
Soul Barnacles: Ten More Years with Ray (edited by Greg Simon)
A Concert of Tenses: Essays on Poetry
Carver Country (photographs by Bob Adelman, introduction
by Tess Gallagher)
A New Path to the Waterfall (Raymond Carver, introduction
by Tess Gallagher)
All of Us (Raymond Carver, introduction by Tess Gallagher)

TRANSLATION

A Path to the Sea: Poems by Liliana Ursu (with Adam J. Sorkin and
the poet, translator's note by Tess Gallagher)
The Sky behind the Forest: Selected Poems by Liliana Ursu
(with Adam J. Sorkin and the poet)

MIDNIGHT LANTERN

New & Selected Poems

Tess Gallagher

Graywolf Press

Instructions to the Double was originally published by Graywolf Press in 1976. *Under Stars* was originally published by Graywolf Press in 1978. *Willingly* was originally published by Graywolf Press in 1984. *Amplitude: New and Selected Poems* was originally published by Graywolf Press in 1987. *Moon Crossing Bridge* was originally published by Graywolf Press in 1992. *Portable Kisses* was originally published by Capra Press in 1994. *My Black Horse: New and Selected Poems* was originally published in Britain by Bloodaxe Books in 1995. *Dear Ghosts,* was originally published by Graywolf Press in 2006.

This publication is made possible by funding provided in part by a grant from the Minnesota State Arts Board, through an appropriation by the Minnesota State Legislature, a grant from the National Endowment for the Arts, and private funders. Significant support has also been provided by Target; the McKnight Foundation; and other generous contributions from foundations, corporations, and individuals. To these organizations and individuals we offer our heartfelt thanks.

Published by Graywolf Press
250 Third Avenue North, Suite 600
Minneapolis, Minnesota 55401

www.graywolfpress.org

Published in the United States of America
Printed in Canada

ISBN 978-1-55597-597-5

2 4 6 8 9 7 5 3 1
First Graywolf Printing, 2011

Library of Congress Control Number: 2011930485

Cover design: Kyle G. Hunter

Cover art: Josie Gray, *Moon's Star-Home*
Photo by Brian Farrell

Contents

from Dear Ghosts, (2006)

Signature: New Poems (2011)

. . . Stars—
Such a plaintive, farewell hissing
they made, like diamonds imbedded
in the blue-black breast of forever.

T. G.
"LAUGHTER AND STARS"

Like a thumb print
on glass, you hover
in daylight, marking the sky
with a scar of midnight.

T. G.
"MOON'S RAINBOW BODY"

from

Instructions to the Double

1976

Even though images in the pool
seem so blurry:
grasp the main thing.
Only in the double kingdom, there
alone, do voices become
undying and tender.

RAINER MARIA RILKE
(TRANSLATED BY ROBERT BLY)

WHEN YOU SPEAK TO ME

Take care when you speak to me.
I might listen, I might
draw near as the flame
breathing with the log, breathing
with the tree it has not
forgotten. I might
put my face
next to
your face
in your nameless trouble,
in your trouble
and name.

It is a thing I learned
without learning; a hand
is a stronger mouth, a kiss could
crack the skull, these
words, small steps
in the air calling
the secret hands, the mouths
hidden in the flesh.

This isn't robbery.
This isn't your blood for my
tears, no confidence
in trade or barter. I may
say nothing back
which is to hear
after you the fever
inside the words we say
apart, the words we say so hard
they fall apart.

INSTRUCTIONS TO THE DOUBLE

So now it's your turn,
little mother of silences, little
father of half-belief. Take up
this face, these daily rounds
with a cabbage under each arm
convincing the multitudes
that a well-made-anything
could save them. Take up
most of all, these hands
trained to an ornate piano
in a house on the other side
of the country.

I'm staying here
without music, without
applause. I'm not going
to wait up for you. Take
your time. Take mine
too. Get into some trouble
I'll have to account for. Walk
into some bars alone
with a slit in your skirt. Let
the men follow you on the street
with their clumsy propositions, their
loud hatreds of this and that. Keep
walking. Keep your head
up. They are calling to you—slut, mother,
virgin, whore, daughter, adulteress, lover,
mistress, bitch, wife, cunt, harlot,
betrothed, Jezebel, Messalina, Diana,
Bathsheba, Rebecca, Lucretia, Mary,

Magdelena, Ruth, you—Niobe,
woman of the tombs.

Don't stop for anything, not
a caress or a promise. Go
to the temple of the poets, not
the one like a run-down country club,
but the one on fire
with so much it wants
to be done with. Say all the last words
and the first: hello, goodbye, yes,
I, no, please, always, never.

If anyone from the country club
asks you to write poems, say
your name is Lizzie Borden.
Show him your axe, the one
they gave you with a silver
blade, your name engraved there
like a whisper of their own.

If anyone calls you a witch,
burn for him; if anyone calls you
less or more than you are
let him burn for you.

It's a dangerous mission. You
could die out there. You
could live forever.

Beginning to Say No

is not to offer so much as a fist, is
to walk away firmly, as though
you had settled something foolish,
is to wear a tarantula in your buttonhole
yet smile invitingly, unmindful
how your own blood grows toward the irreversible
bite. No, I will not

go with you. No, that is not
all right. I'm not your sweet-dish, your
home-cooking, good-looking daf-
fodil. Yes is no
reason to slay the Cyclops. No
will not save it. And the cricket, "Yes, yes."

Fresh bait, fresh bait!
The search for the right hesitation
includes finally
unobstructed waters. Goodbye,
old happy-go-anyhow, old shoe
for any weather. Whose
candelabra are you? Whose
soft-guy, nevermind, nothing-to-lose anthill?

"And," the despised connective,
is really an engine
until it is *yes* all day, until a light
is thrown against a wall
with some result. And
there is less doubt, yes or no,
for whatever you have been compelled to say
more than once.

BREASTS

The day you came
this world got its hold on me.
Summer grass and the four of us pounding hell
out of each other for god knows what
green murder of the skull.
Swart nubbins, I noticed you then,
my mother shaking a gritty rag from the porch
to get my shirt on this minute. Brothers,
that was the parting of our ways, for then
you got me down by something else than flesh.
By the loose skin of a cotton shirt
you kept me to the ground
until the bloody gout hung in my face like a web.

Little mothers, I can't find your children.
I have looked in a man
who moved through the air like a god.
He brought me clouds
and the loose stars of his goings.
Another kissed me on a pier in Georgia
but there was blood on his hands,
bad whiskey in the wind. The last one,
he made me a liar until I stole
what I could not win. Loves,
what is this mirror you have left me in?

I could have told you at the start
there would be trouble
from other hands, how the sharp mouths
would find you where you slept.
But I have hurt you as certainly

with cold sorrowing as anyone,
have come the long way
over broken ground to this softness.
Good clowns, how could I know, all along
it was your blundering mercies kept me alive
when heaven was a luckless dream.

THE WOMAN WHO RAISED GOATS

Dear ones, in those days it was otherwise.
I was suited more to an obedience
of windows. If anyone had asked,
I would have said: "Windows are my prologue."

My father worked on the docks
in a cold little harbor, unhappily
dedicated to what was needed
by the next and further
harbors. My brothers
succeeded him in this, but when I,
in that town's forsaken luster, offered myself,
the old men in the hiring hall creeled
back in their chairs, fanning themselves
with their cards, with their gloves.
"Saucy," they said. "She's saucy!"

Denial, O my Senators,
takes a random shape. The matter
drove me to wearing
a fedora. Soon, the gowns, the amiable
forgeries: a powdery sailor, the blue silk
pillow given by a great aunt, my name
embroidered on it like a ship, the stitched
horse too, with its red plume and its bird eyes
glowing. There was the education
of my "sensibilities."

All this is nothing to you.
You have eaten my only dress, and the town
drifts every day now

toward the harbor. But always,
above the town, above
the harbor, there is the town,
the harbor, the caves and hollows
when the cargo of lights
is gone.

BLACK MONEY

His lungs heaving all day in a sulphur mist,
then dusk, the lunch pail torn from him
before he reaches the house, his children
a cloud of swallows about him.
At the stove in the tumbled rooms, the wife,
her back the wall he fights most, and she
with no weapon but silence
and to keep him from the bed.

In their sleep the mill hums and turns
at the edge of water. Blue smoke
swells the night and they drift
from the graves they have made for each other,
float out from the open-mouthed sleep
of their children, past banks and businesses,
the used car lots, liquor store, the swings in the park.

The mill burns on, now a burst of cinders,
now whistles screaming down the bay, saws jagged
in half-light. Then like a whip
the sun across the bed, windows high with mountains
and the sleepers fallen to pillows
as gulls fall, tilting
against their shadows on the log booms.
Again the trucks shudder the wood-framed houses
passing to the mill. My father
snorts, splashes in the bathroom,
throws open our doors to cowboy music
on the radio. Hearts are cheating,
somebody is alone, there's blood in Tulsa.
Out the back yard the night-shift men rattle

the gravel in the alley going home.
My father fits goggles to his head.

From his pocket he takes anything metal,
the pearl-handled jack knife, a ring of keys,
and for us, black money shoveled
from the sulphur pyramids heaped in the distance
like yellow gold. Coffee bottle tucked in his armpit
he swaggers past the chicken coop,
a pack of cards at his breast.
In a fan of light beyond him
the *Kino Maru* pulls out for Seattle,
some black star climbing
the deep globe of his eye.

KIDNAPER

He motions me over with a question.
He is lost. I believe him. It seems
he calls my name. I move
closer. He says it again, the name
of someone he loves. I step back pretending

not to hear. I suspect
the street he wants
does not exist, but I am glad to point
away from myself. While he turns
I slip off my wristwatch, already laying a trail
for those who must find me
tumbled like an abandoned car
into the ravine. I lie

without breath for days among ferns.
Pine needles drift
onto my face and breasts
like the tiny hands
of watches. Cars pass.
I imagine it's him
coming back. My death
is not needed. The sun climbs again
for everyone. He lifts me
like a bride

and the leaves fall from my shoulders
in twenty-dollar bills.
"You must have been cold," he says
covering me with his handkerchief.
"You must have given me up."

STEPPING OUTSIDE

for Akhmatova

Hearing of you, I never lost a brother
though I have, never saw a husband to war,
though I have, never kept with my father
the emptiness of his hands, my mother
the dying of her womb.

Return: husbands, sons, fathers return.
Many with both arms, with dreams
broken in both eyes.
They try, they try
but they cannot tell us
what comes back with them.

One more has planted his hoe
in my heart like an axe, my farmer uncle
slain by thieves
in the night, burned down
with his house, buried, dug up
to prove he was no dog.
He was no dog.

You, who lived in your pain until it grew
its own face, would have left all this
like a monument in a field. Your words
would have made a feast of what ate you.

Sit with me.
No one has left; no one returns.

Two Stories

(To the author of a story taken from the death of my uncle, Porter Morris, murdered June 7, 1972, Windyville, Missouri)

You kept the names, the flies
of who they were, mine
gone carnival, ugly Tessie.
It got wilder but nothing
personal. The plot had me
an easy lay for a buck.
My uncle came to life
as my lover. At 16
the murderer stabbed cows
and mutilated chickens. Grown,
you gave him a crowbar that happened
to be handy twice. Then you made him
do it alone. For me
it took three drunks, a gun, the house
on fire. There was a black space
between trees where I told you.

The shape of my uncle
spread its arms on the wire springs
in the yard and the neighbors
came to look at his shadow
caught there under the nose
of his dog. They left that angel
to you. Your killer never
mentioned money. Like us he wanted
to outlive his hand in the sure blood
of another. The veins of my uncle streaked
where the house had been. They watched

until morning. Your man found a faucet
in an old man's side. His pants
were stiff with it for days. He left
the crowbar on Tessie's porch like a bone.

My weapon was never found.
The murderers drove a white
station wagon and puked
as they went. They hoped
for 100 dollar bills stuffed
in a lard can. But a farmer
keeps his money in cattle
and land. They threw his billfold
into the ditch like an empty
bird. One ran away. Two stayed
with women. I kept the news
blind. You took it from my mouth,
shaped it for the market, still
a dream worse than I remembered.

Now there is the story of me
reading your story and the one
of you saying it
doesn't deserve such care.
I say it matters
that the dog stays by the chimney
for months, and a rain
soft as the sleep of cats
enters the land, emptied
of its cows, its wire gates pulled down
by hands that never dug
the single well, this whitened field.

The Calm

We were walking through the bees
and stars. Our mouths
made a sense without us.
I loved your hands
because of your mouth, each star
because of a life not chosen
by the hand. I told you,
don't say it, the loss
of our lives beyond us. You
said it. You said it
for the sake of a loneliness
together, for the praise of our eyes
going on without shadows.

Even now, when all our nights
have washed away
and the apples have left
the trees, I am keeping your place
where the high grass
has entered the song. Like a swarm,
the heart moves with its separate
wings under the eaves.

If I knew where to find you
I would say good-bye
and have the hurtful ease of that,
but the gates are everywhere
and this calm—an imagined forgiveness,
the childhood before we meet again.

CORONA

Personable shadow, you follow me into this
daylight-dream, the one even my body
knows nothing of.

This flesh is your halo, the meat you drag daily
across the earth like an injured
wife. The sun

surrounds us as the heart surrounds
the body. Let us
navigate each pleasure, each pain

like a doorway, its ambush: the mouth, the bouquet,
the six-story ladder, that
memory of a train

missed in Budapest, everything passing through.
The tail of a shirt
caresses the back of my brother who falls again

from the tractor in 1957. A woman's body
flies out of the house
like an insult. It is the day we are found

missing. See
the windows floating beside us into the next world,
admitting they don't know what they're for.

I will speak to you like a lover, not as one
I have used
to keep from being true. This water is a memory

of sleep folding us
under. Your face
covers mine; the moon of your face blasted from a train

through faults of light in the trees—again and
again cut off, this water
taking up our hands.

SNOWHEART

In our houses, the snow keeps us
traveling. It says: your life
is where you are. The phone,
all day ringing by itself
over the next lot, isn't for you.

The man with the perfect
haircut makes a track
across the lawn, holding
his books like a
breast. *Snowheart*

you have said: *don't cut your black hair.*

Love's the only debt.
He's up again
and riding the best mare
ten miles by moonlight, the
spruce-backed fiddle
under his arm.

"Dance us the next one too.
If day comes, don't
tell. Let the horse
go home alone."

Snowheart. Someone's horse
circles the near house.
There is snow
on its back.

COMING HOME

As usual, I was desperate.
I went through your house as if I owned it.
I said, "I need This, This and This."
But contrary to all I know of you,
you did not answer, only looked after me.

I've never seen the house so empty, Mother.
Even the rugs felt it, how little
they covered. And what have you done
with the plants? How thankfully
we thought their green replaced us.

You were keeping something like a light.
I had seen it before, a place you'd never been
or never came back from. It was a special way
your eyes looked out over the water. Whitecaps
lifted the bay and you said, "He should be here
by now."

How he always came back; the drinking,
the fishing into the night, all
the ruthless ships he unloaded.
That was the miracle of our lives. Even now
he won't stay out of what I have
to say to you.

But they worry me, those boxes
of clothes I left in your basement. Sometimes
I think of home as a storehouse, the more
we leave behind, the less
you say. The last time
I couldn't take anything.

So I'm always coming back like tonight,
in a temper, brushing the azaleas
on the doorstep. What did you mean
by it, this tenderness
that is a whip, a longing?

RHODODENDRONS

Like porches they trust their attachments,
or seem to, the road and the trees
leaving them open from both sides.
I have admired their spirit,
wild-headed women of the roadside,
how exclusion is only something glimpsed,
the locomotive dream that learns to go on
without caring for the landscape.

There is a spine in the soil
I have not praised enough:
its underhair of surface
clawed to the air. Elsewhere each shore
recommends an ease of boats, shoulders
nodding over salmon
who cross this sky with our faces.

I was justifying my confusion
the last time we walked this way.
I think I said some survivals need
a forest. But it was only the sound
of knowing. Assumptions
about roots put down like a deeper foot
seemed dangerous too.

These were flowers you did not cut,
iris and mums a kindness enough.
Some idea of relative dignities, I suppose,
let us spare each other; I came away
with your secret consent and this
lets you stand like a grief
telling itself over and over.

Even grief has instructions,
like the boats gathering light
from the water and the separate
extensions of the roots. So remembering
is only one more way of being alone
when the voice has gone everywhere
in the dusk of the porches
looking for the last thing to say.

for my mother

from

Under Stars

1978

What Cathál Said

You can sing sweet
and get the song sung
but to get to the third dimension
you have to sing it
rough, hurt the tune a little. Put
enough strength to it
that the notes slip. Then
something else happens. The song
gets large.

T. G.

. . . to be under another appearance . . . that, I think,
is poetry.

SEAN O'RIORDAN
(TRANSLATED BY CIARAN CARSON)

Women's Tug of War at Lough Arrow

In a borrowed field they dig in their feet
and clasp the rope. Balanced
against neighboring women, they hold
the ground by the little gained
and, leaning like boatmen rowing into
the damp earth, they pull
to themselves the invisible waves, waters
overcalmed by desertion
or the narrow look trained to a brow.

The steady rain has made girls of them,
their hair in ringlets. Now they haul
the live weight to the cries
of husbands and children, until the rope
runs slack, runs free
and all are bound again by the arms
of those who held them, not until, but so
they gave.

ON YOUR OWN

How quickly the postures shift.
Just moments ago we seemed human,
or in the Toledo of my past
I made out I was emotionally illiterate
so as not to feel a pain I deserved.

Here at the Great Southern
some of the boys have made it
into gray suits and pocket calculators.
I'm feeling end-of-season, like a somebody
who's hung around the church
between a series of double weddings.

Friend, what you said about the terror
of American Womanhood,
I forget it already, but I know
what you mean. I'm so scary some days
I'd run from myself. It's hard work
having your way, even
half the time, and having it,
know what not to do with it. Who
hasn't thrown away a life or two
at the mercy of another's passion,
spite or industry.

It's like this on your own: the charms
unlucky, the employment
solitary, the best love always
the benefit of a strenuous doubt.

WOMAN-ENOUGH

Figures on a silent screen,
they move into my window, its facing
on the abbey yard, six men with spades
and long-handled shovels. I had looked up
as I look up now across the strand where a small boat
has drifted into the haze of mountains
or that child walks to the end
of a dock.

Both views let in sun.
The bearded one throws off his coat
and rolls his sleeves. Two in their best clothes
from offices in London lean against a stone,
letting the shovels lift and slap.
The others dodge in and out of sun, elbow-high,
the ground thickening. The boat,
closer, one oar flashing,

pulled to the light and under, these voices
a darker blade. A wind
carries over and I hear him call out to me: "He
was a wild one in his young days. You'll want
to lock your door." He nods the bottle
to bring me out.

A drink to you, Peter Harte, man
that I never knew, lover
of cattle and one good woman
buried across the lake.
"He was a tall man, about my size," the one
measuring, face down in the gap.

"And wouldn't you like a big man? Big
as me?" dusting his hands on his trousers and lifted out.

The boat head-on now
so it stays.

"Try it on, go down."

The sky, the stone blue
of the sky. An edge of faces, hard looks
as though they'd hauled me live
into the open boat of their deaths, American woman,
man-enough in that country place
to stand with skulls sifted and stacked
beside the dirt pile, but woman then
where none had stood and them more men
for that mistake to see me
where he would lay.

"Not a word of this to Mary, ye hear."

O he was a wild one,
a wild one in his youth, Sonny Peter
Harte.

The Ritual of Memories

When your widow had left the graveside
and you were most alone
I went to you in that future
you can't remember yet. I brought
a basin of clear water where no tear
had fallen, water gathered like grapes
a drop at a time
from the leaves of the willow. I brought
oils, I brought a clean white gown.

"Come out," I said, and you came up
like a man pulling himself out of a river,
a river with so many names
there was no word left for it but 'earth'.

"Now," I said, "I'm ready. These eyes
that have not left your face
since the day we met, wash these eyes.
Remember, it was a country road
above the sea and I was passing
from the house of a friend. Look
into these eyes where we met."

I saw your mind go back through the years
searching for that day and finding it,
you washed my eyes
with the pure water
so that I vanished from that road
and you passed a lifetime
and I was not there.

So you washed every part of me
where any look or touch
had passed between us. "Remember,"
I said, when you came to the feet,
"it was the night before you would ask
the girl of your village to marry. I
was the strange one. I was the one
with the gypsy look.
Remember how you stroked these feet."

When the lips and the hands
had been treated likewise and the pit
of the throat where one thoughtless kiss
had fallen, you rubbed in the sweet oil
and I glistened like a new-made thing, not
merely human, but of the world gone past
being human.

"The hair," I said. "You've forgotten
the hair. Don't you know it remembers.
Don't you know it keeps everything. Listen,
there is your voice and in it the liar's charm
that caught me."

You listened. You heard your voice
and a look of such sadness
passed over your dead face that I wanted
to touch you. Who could have known
I would be so held? Not you
in your boyish cunning; not me
in my traveler's clothes.

It's finished.
Put the gown on my shoulders.
It's no life in the shadow of another's joys.
Let me go freely now.
One life I have lived for you. This one
is mine.

The Ballad of Ballymote

We stopped at her hut
on the road to Ballymote
but she did not look up
and her head was on her knee.

What is it, we asked.
As from the dreams of the dead
her voice came up.

My father, they shot him
as he looked up from his plate
and again as he stood and again
as he fell against the stove
and like a thrush his breath
bruised the room
and was gone.

A traveler would have asked directions
but saw she would not lift her face.
What is it, he asked.

My husband sits all day in a pub
and all night and I may as well
be a widow for the way he beats me
to prove he's alive.

What is it, asked the traveler's wife,
just come up to look.

My son's lost both eyes in a fight
to keep himself a man

and there he sits behind the door
where there is no door
and he sees by the stumps
of his hands.

And have you no daughters for comfort?

Two there are and gone to nuns
and a third to the North
with a fisherman.

What are you cooking?

Cabbage and bones, she said. Cabbage
and bones.

Disappearances in the Guarded Sector

When we stop where you lived, the house
has thickened, the entry
level to the wall with bricks, as though
it could keep you out.

Again the dream has fooled you into waking
and we have walked out
past ourselves, through the windows
to be remembered in the light
of closed rooms
as a series of impositions
across the arms of a chair, that woman's face
startled out of us so it lingers
along a brick front.

You are leading me back to the burned arcade
where you said I stood with you
in your childhood last night, your childhood
which includes me now
as surely as the look of that missing face
between the rows of houses.

We have gone so far into your past
that nothing reflects us.
No sun gleams from the glassless frame
where a room burned,
though the house stayed whole. There
is your school, your church,
the place you drank cider at lunch time.
New rows of houses are going up.
Children play quietly in a stairwell.

Walking back, you tell the story
of the sniper's bullet
making two clean holes in the taxi, how
the driver ducked and drove on
like nothing happened. No pain
passed through you; it
did not even stop the car
or make you live more
carefully. Near the check point we
stop talking, you let the hands
rub your clothes
against your body. You seem to be
there, all there.

Watching, I am more apart
for the sign of dismissal they will give me,
thinking a woman would not conceal,
as I have, the perfect map
of this return where I have met
and lost you willingly
in a dead and living place.

Now when you find me next in the dream,
this boundary will move with us.
We will both come back.

Belfast. Winter, 1976

OPEN FIRE NEAR A SHED

In the cab there was a song.
Not one I would have chosen, but
of which I remember, in my way,
some words without the tune. Also,
the driver, his coat. How is it
that the wrinkles in his coat-back
were almost tender? His small hands
taking from yours
my belongings.

You're stepping back now
behind the gray slats
of the gate. Your hand, the right
one, lifts through
the fine rain, causing me
to look back at myself
as your memory—a constancy
with its troubled interior
under the rained-on glass.

Looking out, I've moved already
into thought. The tunnel
on the train gives and returns my face
flickering across the winter fields,
the fields—their soft holdings
of water, of cows breathing warmly
over the tracks of birds.

Sudden then as light to the pane—
an open fire near a shed,

wilder in the stubble and light rain
for how it seems intended
to burn there
though no one is standing by.

LOVE POEM TO BE READ TO
AN ILLITERATE FRIEND

I have had to write this down
in my absence and yours. These
things happen. Thinking
of a voice added
I imagine a sympathy outside us
that protects the message
from what can't help
being said.

The times you've kept
your secret, putting on
glasses or glancing into a page
with interest, give again
the hurt you've forgiven, pretending
to be one of us.
So the hope of love
translates as a series of hidden moments
where we like to think
someone was fooled
into it.

Who was I then
who filled these days
with illegible warnings: the marriages
broken, the land
pillaged by speculators, no word
for a stranger?

This island
where I thought the language mine

has left me lonely
and innocent as you or that friend
who let you copy his themes
until the words became pictures
of places you would never go.

Forgive it then
that so much of after
depends on these, the words
which must find you
off the page.

SECOND LANGUAGE

Outside, the night is glowing
with earth and rain, and you
in the next room take up
your first language.
All day it has waited
like a young girl in a field.
Now she has stood up
from the straw-flattened circle
and you have taken her glance
from the hills.

The words come back.
You are with yourself again
as that child who gave up the spoon,
the bed, the horse to its colors
and uses. There is yet no hint
they would answer to anything else
and your tongue does not multiply the wrong,
the stammer calling them back
and back.

You have started the one word
again, again as though it had to be made
a letter at a time
until it mends itself into saying.
The girl is beside you as lover or mother or
the aunt who visited with a kindly face
and the story of your mother
as a girl in a life before you.

She leads you across that field
to where the cows put down their wet lips
to the rust-dry trough.
But before you can get there
it will have changed. The water
will have two names
in and out of the ground. The song
you are singing, its familiar words and measures,
will be shadowed and bridged.

Remember the tune for the words.
Remember the cows for the field, those
in their sacred look who return
their great heads to the centuries of grass.

Out of sleep you are glad
for this rain, are steadied by my staying awake.
The trough will fill
and it will seem as though the dream
completes its far side.

To speak is to be robbed and clothed,
this language always mine
because so partly yours. Each word
has a crack in it to show the strain
of all it holds, all that leaks
away. Silent now, as when another
would think you sullen or
absent, you smoke after a meal, the sign
of food still on the plate, the two
chairs drawn away and angled again
into the room.

The rain enters, repeating its single word
until our bodies in their store-bought clothes
make a sound against us, the dangerous visit
of the flesh perfecting its fears
and celebrations, drinking us in
by the slow unspeakable syllables.

I have forced up the screen
and put out the palm of my hand past the rush
of the eaves. In the circular glow of the porch
the lighted rain is still, is falling.

for Ciaran

EVER AFTER

Exactly like a rain cloud
over the picnickers at the abbey
or a boat reflecting
on the peak of itself without an oar, so
my death reached everything in my mind
effortlessly.

This amazed my normal appearance,
which went on swallowing
an excessive quantity of rain. An odd
expression of joy. Great sheets
of rain. Then passing

I caught the words of the mourners
like a skirt waving backwards on a scarlet road
and among them, the girl who would lie
beside me.

The long-handled shovel
from dawn to dark like a machine
and she one soft touch
for the gulls to swoop at. Cloth
buttons.

We looked at the red lights
wandering over the masts of the ships,
their dark facings in the brain,
the trees climbing side by side
with the sky into that exchange of worlds, her
hair flowing over
the river-wall. Her life, she said,

an imaginary bird let go in the white water
of January. Water that lapped
the doorstep, her short legs, her hand
on the window sill near the bridge, near
the look of the gulls
floating between the timbers.

Closing the fact of it, think
of her dead, think of a skeleton
you could embrace as the lack
of your being or lying
in this field to talk through the cry of water
into the whole future
which brings back the hands
free and ready. Think

of her. That's better. She
was at my side, the memory of her. The
wetness of the sea. I
explained to her: because you are alive
the horizon recedes. You thought you were
everything, a drum with affection, the sort
of girl to mark that page
because one hand held another
or you could skip it altogether.

If I were everything, there would be nothing
beside me. You
are beside me. The sort of girl

she was, looking out at me
through the lattices
of her hair, her
live hair.

My Mother Remembers That She Was Beautiful

for Georgia Morris (Quigley) Bond

The falling snow has made her thoughtful
and young in the privacy
of our table with its netted candle
and thick white plates. The serious faces
of the lights breathe on the pine boards
behind her. She is visiting
the daughter never close
or far enough away to come to.

She keeps her coat on, called into
her girlhood by such forgetting
I am gone or yet
to happen. She sees herself
among the townspeople, the country glances
slow with fields and sky
as she passes or waits
with a brother in the hot animal smell
of the auction stand: sunlight,
straw hats, a dog's tail
brushing her bare leg.

"There are things you know.
I didn't have to beg," she said, "for anything."

The beautiful one speaks to me
from the changed, proud face and I see
how little I've let her know
of what she becomes. Years

were never the trouble, or the white hair
I braided near the sea
on a summer day. Who
she must have been
is lost to me through some fault
in my own reflection and we will have to go on
as we think we are, walking for no one's sake
from the empty restaurant into the one color
of the snow—before us, the close houses,
the brave and wondering lights of the houses.

UNDER STARS

The sleep of this night deepens
because I have walked coatless from the house
carrying the white envelope.
All night it will say one name
in its little tin house by the roadside.

I have raised the metal flag
so its shadow under the roadlamp
leaves an imprint on the rain-heavy bushes.
Now I will walk back
thinking of the few lights still on
in the town a mile away.

In the yellowed light of a kitchen
the millworker has finished his coffee,
his wife has laid out the white slices of bread
on the counter. Now while the bed they have left
is still warm, I will think of you, you
who are so far away
you have caused me to look up at the stars.

Tonight they have not moved
from childhood, those games played after dark.
Again I walk into the wet grass
toward the starry voices. Again, I
am the found one, intimate, returned
by all I touch on the way.

from

Willingly

1984

> *So does*
> *a bird dismiss one tree for another*
> *and carries each time the flight between*
> *like a thing never done.*
> *And what is proof then, but some trance*
> *to kill the birds?*

T. G.
"CANDLE, LAMP & FIREFLY"

SUDDEN JOURNEY

Maybe I'm seven in the open field—
the straw-grass so high
only the top of my head makes a curve
of brown in the yellow. Rain then.
First a little. A few drops on my
wrist, the right wrist. More rain.
My shoulders, my chin. Until I'm looking up
to let my eyes take the bliss.
I open my face. Let the teeth show. I
pull my shirt down past the collarbones.
I'm still a boy under my breast spots.
I can drink anywhere. The rain. My
skin shattering. Up suddenly, needing
to gulp, turning with my tongue, my arms out
running, running in the hard, cold plenitude
of all those who reach earth by falling.

UNSTEADY YELLOW

I went to the field to break
and to bury my precious things.
I went to the field
with a sack and a spade,
to the cool field alone.

All that he gave me
I dashed and I covered.
The glass horse, the necklace,
the live bird with its song, with
its wings like two harps—
in the ground, in the damp ground.

Its song, when I snatched it again
to air, flung it with light
over the tall new corn, its pure joy
must have reached him.

In a day it was back, my freed bird
was back. Oh now, what will I do,
what will I do with its song
on my shoulder, with its heart
on my shoulder when we come to
the field, to the high yellow field?

FROM DREAD IN THE EYES OF HORSES

Eggs. Dates and camel's milk.
Give this. In one hour the foal will
stand, in two will run. The care then of
women, the schooling from fear, clamor
of household, a prospect of saddles.

They kneel to it, folded
on its four perfect legs, stroke
the good back, the muscles bunched at the chest.
Its head, how the will shines large in it
as what may be used to overcome it.

The women of the horses comb out
their cruel histories of hair only for
the pleasure of horses, for the lost mares
on the Ridge of Yellow Horses, their white arms
praying the hair down breasts ordinary

as knees. The extent of their power,
this intimation of sexual wealth. From dread
in the eyes of horses are taken their songs.
In the white forests the last free horses
eat branches and roots, are hunted like deer
and carry no one.

A wedge of light where the doorway opens
the room—in it, a sickness of sleep.
The arms of the women, their coarse
white hair. In a bank of sunlight, a man
whitewashes the house he owns—no shores, no
worlds above it and farther, shrill, obsidian,
the high feasting of the horses.

Death of the Horses by Fire

We have seen a house in the sleeping town
stand still for a fire and the others,
where their windows knew it,
clothed in the remnants of a dream
happening outside them. We have seen
the one door aflame in the many windows,
the steady procession of the houses
trembling in heat-light, their well-tended
yards, the trellis of cabbage roses scrawled
against the porch—flickering white, whiter
where a darkness breathes back.

How many nights the houses have burned through
to morning. We stood in our blankets
like a tribe made to witness
what a god could do.

We saw the house built again in daylight
and children coming from it
as what a house restores to itself in rooms
so bright they do not forget, even
when the father, when the mother
dies. "Kitchen of your childhoods!" we shout
at the old men alive on the benches
in the square. Their good, black eyes
glitter back at us, a star-fall
of homecomings.

Only when the horses began to burn
in the funnel of light hurrying in one place
on the prairie did we begin to suspect

our houses, to doubt at our meals
and pleasures. We gathered on the ridge
above the horses, above the blue smoke
of the grasses, and they whirled in the close
circle of the death that came to them, rippling in
like a deep moon to its water. With
the hills in all directions
they stood in the last of their skies
and called to each other to save them.

3 A.M. KITCHEN: MY FATHER TALKING

For years it was land working me, oil fields,
cotton fields, then I got some land. I
worked it. Them days you could just about
make a living. I was logging.

Then I sent to Missouri. Momma
come out. We got married.
We got some kids. Five kids.
That kept us going.

We bought some land near the water.
It was cheap then. The water
was right there. You just looked out
the window. It never left the window.

I bought a boat. Fourteen footer.
There was fish out there then.
You remember, we used to catch
six, eight fish, clean them right
out in the yard. I could of fished to China.

I quit the woods. One day just
walked out, took off my caulks, said that's
it. I went to the docks.
I was driving winch. You had to watch
to see nothing fell out of the sling. If
you killed somebody you'd
never forget it. All
those years I was just working
I was on edge, every day. Just working.

You kids. I could tell you
a lot. But I won't.

It's winter. I play a lot of cards
down at the tavern. Your mother.
I have to think of excuses
to get out of the house. You're
wasting your time, she says. You're wasting
your money.

You don't have no idea, Threasie.
I run out of things
to work for. Hell, why shouldn't I
play cards? Threasie,
some days now I just don't know.

ACCOMPLISHMENT

What not to do for him
was hardest, for the life left in us
argued against his going
like a moon banished in fullness, yet
lingering far into morning, pale
with new light, gradually a view of
mountains, a sea emerging—its prickly
channels and dark shelves
breeding in the violet morning. Ships too,
after a while. Some anchored, others
moving by degree, as if to leave without affront
this harbor, a thin shoal curved like an arm—
ever embracing, ever releasing.

He too was shaped to agreement, the hands
no longer able to hold, at rest
on the handmade coverlet. His tongue
arched forward in the open mouth where breath
on breath he labored, the task beyond all strength
so the body shuddered like a chill
on the hinge of his effort, then rose again.

After a time, we saw the eyes gaze upward
without appeal—eyes without knowing or need
of knowing. Some in the room began to
plead, as if he meant to take them with him,
and they were afraid. A daughter bent near,
calling his name, then gave her own,
firmly, like a dock he might cling to.
The breath eased, then drifted momentarily,
considering or choosing, we did not know.

"At some point we have to let him go."
"I know," she said. "I know."

In the last moments the eyes widened and,
with the little strength left, he
strained upward and toward. "He had to be
looking *at* something. You don't look
at nothing that way." Not
pain, but some sharpening beyond
the visible. Not eagerness or surprise, but
as though he would die in time to intercept
an onrushing world, for which
he had prepared himself
with that dead face.

Black Silk

She was cleaning—there is always
that to do—when she found,
at the top of the closet, his old
silk vest. She called me
to look at it, unrolling it carefully
like something live
might fall out. Then we spread it
on the kitchen table and smoothed
the wrinkles down, making our hands
heavy until its shape against Formica
came back and the little tips
that would have pointed to his pockets
lay flat. The buttons were all there.
I held my arms out and she
looped the wide armholes over
them. "That's one thing I never
wanted to be," she said, "a man."
I went into the bathroom to see
how I looked in the sheen and
sadness. Wind chimes
off-key in the alcove. Then her
crying so I stood back in the sink-light
where the porcelain had been staring. Time
to go to her, I thought, with that
other mind, and stood still.

CANDLE, LAMP & FIREFLY

How can I think what thoughts
to have of you with a mind so unready?
What I remember most: you did not want
to go. Then choice slipped from you
like snow from the mountain, so death
could graze you over with the sweet
muzzles of the deer moving up from
the valleys, pausing to stare
down and back toward the town. But you
did not gaze back. Like a cut rose
on the fifth day, you bowed
into yourself and we watched the shell-
shaped petals drop in clumps, then,
like wine, deepen into the white cloth.

What have you written here on my sleep
with flesh so sure I have no choice
but to stare back when your face and
gestures follow me into daylight?
Your arms, too weak at your death
for embracing, closed around me and held,
and such a tenderness was mixed there
with longing that I asked, "Is it good
where you are?"

We echoed a long time in the kiss
that was drinking me—*daughter, daughter,
daughter*—until I was gone as when a sun
drops over the rim of an ocean, gone
yet still there. Then the dampness,
the chill of your body pulled from me

into that space the condemned
look back to after parting.

Between sleep and death
I carry no proof that we met, no proof
but to tell what even I must call dream
and gently dismiss. So does
a bird dismiss one tree for another
and carries each time the flight between
like a thing never done.
And what is proof then, but some trance
to kill the birds? And what are dreams
when the eyes open on similar worlds
and you are dead in my living?

THE HUG

A woman is reading a poem on the street
and another woman stops to listen. We stop too,
with our arms around each other. The poem
is being read and listened to out here
in the open. Behind us
no one is entering or leaving the houses.

Suddenly a hug comes over me and I'm
giving it to you, like a variable star shooting light
off to make itself comfortable, then
subsiding. I finish but keep on holding
you. A man walks up to us and we know he hasn't
come out of nowhere, but if he could, he
would have. He looks homeless because of how
he needs. "Can I have one of those?" he asks you,
and I feel you nod. I'm surprised,
surprised you don't tell him how
it is—that I'm yours, only
yours, etc., exclusive as a nose to
its face. Love—that's what we're talking about, love
that nabs you with "for me
only" and holds on.

So I walk over to him and put my
arms around him and try to
hug him like I mean it. He's got an overcoat on
so thick I can't feel
him past it. I'm starting the hug
and thinking, "How big a hug is this supposed to be?
How long shall I hold this hug?" Already
we could be eternal, his arms falling over my

shoulders, my hands not
meeting behind his back, he is so big!

I put my head into his chest and snuggle
in. I lean into him. I lean my blood and my wishes
into him. He stands for it. This is his
and he's starting to give it back so well I know he's
getting it. This hug. So truly, so tenderly
we stop having arms and I don't know if
my lover has walked away or what, or
if the woman is still reading the poem, or the houses—
what about them?—the houses.

Clearly a little permission is a dangerous thing.
But when you hug someone you want it
to be a masterpiece of connection, the way the button
on his coat will leave the imprint of
a planet in my cheek
when I walk away. When I try to find some place
to go back to.

WOODCUTTING ON LOST MOUNTAIN

for Leslie and for Morris

Our father is three months dead
from lung cancer and you light another Camel,
ease the chainsaw into the log. You
don't need habits to tell us
you're the one most like him.
Maybe the least loved
carries injury farther into tenderness
for having first to pass through
forgiveness. You
passed through. "I think he respected me
at the end," as if you'd waited a lifetime
to offer yourself that in my listening.

"Top of the mountain!" your daughter cries.
She's ten, taking swigs with us
from the beer can in the January sun. We see
other mountain tops and trees forever.
A mountain *could* get lost in all this, right
enough, even standing on it, thinking this
is where you are.

"Remember the cabins we built when we were
kids? The folks logging Deer Park and
Black Diamond." My brother, Morris, nods,
pulls the nose of the saw into the air as a chunk
falls. "We built one good one. They
brought their lunches and sat with us
inside—Spam sandwiches on white bread,

bananas for dessert and Mountain Bars, white
on the inside, pure sugar on
the inside—the way they hurt your teeth."

Sawdust sprays across his knee, his face
closes in thought. "Those whippings." He
cuts the motor, wipes his forehead with an arm.
"They'd have him in jail today. I used to beg
and run circles. You got it worse because you
never cried. It's a wonder we didn't
run away." "Away to where?" I say. "There's no
away when you're a kid. Before you can get there
you're home."

"Once he took you fishing and left me
behind," my brother says.
"I drew pictures of you sinking
all over the chicken house. I gave you a head
but no arms. We
could go back today and there
they'd be, boats
sinking all down the walls."

His daughter is Leslie, named after our father.
Then I think—'She's a logger's daughter,
just like me'—and the thought pleases as if
the past had intended this present. "You
didn't know you were doing it," I tell him,
"but you figured how to stay
in our childhood." "I guess I did. There's
nothing I'd rather do," he says, "than cut wood.

Look at that—" he points to stacks of logs
high as a house he's thinned from the timber—
"they're going to burn them. Afraid
somebody might take a good tree
for firewood, so they'll burn half a forest.
Damn, that's the Forest Service for you. Me—
I work here, they'll have to stop me."

Leslie carries split wood to the tailgate
and I toss it into the truck. We make
a game of it, trying to stack as fast
as her father cuts. "She's a worker,"
Morris says. "Look at that girl go.
Sonofagun, I wouldn't trade four boys for her.
No sir." He picks up the maul, gives a yell
and whacks down through the center of a block
thick as a man. It falls neatly into
halves. "Look at that! Now *that's* good wood.
That's beautiful wood," he says, like he
made it himself.

I tell him how the cells of trees
are like the blood cells of people, how trees
are the oldest organisms on the earth. Before
the English cut the trees off Ireland, the Irish
had three dozen words for green. He's impressed,
mildly, has his own way of thinking about trees.

Tomorrow a log pile will collapse
on him and he will just get out alive.

"Remember the time Dad felled the tree on us
and Momma saved us, pushed us into a ditch? It's
a wonder we ever grew up."

"One of the horses they logged with, Dick
was his name, Old Dick. They gave him
to Oney Brown and Dick got into the house
while everyone was gone and broke
all the dishes. Dishes—what could they mean
to a horse? Still, I think he knew
what he was doing."

Oney's wife, Sarah, had fifteen kids. She's
the prettiest woman I'll ever see. Her son,
Lloyd, took me down to the railroad tracks
to show me the dead hounds. "We had too many
so they had to shoot some." The hounds were
skeletons by then, but they haven't moved
all these years from the memory
of that dark underneath of boughs.
I look at them, stretched on their sides, twin
arches of bones leaping with beetles and
crawlers into the bark-rich earth. Skipper
and Captain—Cappy for short. Their names
and what seemed incomprehensible—a betrayal
which meant those who had care of you
might, without warning, make an end of you
in some godforsaken, heartless place. Lloyd spat
like a father between the tracks, took
my hand and led me back to the others.

Twenty years settles on the boys
of my childhood. Some of them loggers.
"It's gone," they tell me. "The Boom Days
are gone. We thought
they'd never end, there were
that many trees. But it's finished,
or nearly. Nothing but stumps
and fireweed now."

"Alaska," Morris says, "that's where the trees
are," and I think of them, like some lost tribe
of wanderers, their spires and bloodless blood
climbing cathedral-high into the moss-light
of days on all the lost mountains of
our childhoods.

Coming into the town we see the blue smoke
of the trees streaming like a mystery
the houses hold in common.
"Doesn't seem possible—," he says, "a tree
nothing but a haze you could
put your hand through."

"What'll you do next, after the trees are gone?"

"Pack dudes in for elk."

"Then what?"

"Die, I guess. Hell, I don't know, ask
a shoemaker, ask a salmon . . .
Remember that time I was hunting and got lost,
forgot about the dark and me with no coat, no
compass? You and Dad fired rifles from the road
until I stumbled out. It
was midnight. But I got out. It's a wonder
I could tell an echo from a shot, I was so cold,
so lost. Stop cussing, I told the old man, I'm
home, ain't I? 'You're grown,' he kept saying,
'you're a grown man.'
I must be part wild. I must be part tree or part
deer. I got on the track and I was lost
but it didn't matter. I had to go where it led.
I must be part bobcat."

Leslie is curled under my arm, asleep.

"Truck rocks them to sleep," Morris says.
"Reminds me, I don't have a license for this
piece of junk. I hope I don't get stopped. Look
at her sleep! Right in the middle of the day.
Watch this: 'Wake up honey, we're lost. Help me
get home. You went to sleep and got us lost.'
She must be part butterfly, just look at those eyes.
There—she's gone again. I'll have to carry
her into the house. Happens every time.
Watch her, we'll go up the steps and she'll be
wide awake the minute I open the door.
Hard to believe, we had to be carried into houses
once, you and me. It's a wonder we ever
grew up."

Tomorrow a log pile will collapse
and he'll just get out alive.

He opens the door. Her eyes start,
suddenly awake.

"See, what'd I tell you. Wide awake. Butterfly,
you nearly got us lost, sleeping so long.
Here, walk for yourself. We're home."

GRAY EYES

When she speaks it is like coming onto a grave
   at the edge of a woods, softly, so we
         do not enter or wholly
     turn away. Such speech
is the breath a brush makes through hair,
        opening into time
   after the stroke.

      A tree is bending
but the bird doesn't land.

     One star,
earthbound, reports a multitude of unyielding
  others. It
    cannot help its   falling   falling
into the dull brown earth of someone's back yard,
   where, in daylight, a hand reaches
in front of the mower and tosses it, dead stone,
        aside. We who saw it fall

are still crashing with light into the housetops,
   tracing in the mind that missing
     trajectory, rainbow of darkness
   where we were—children
murmuring—"There, over there!"—while the houses
   slept and slept on.

Years later she is still nesting on the light
   of that plundered moment, her black hair
     frozen to her head with yearning,
   saying, "Father, I am a colder green

where the mower cut a swath
and I lay down

and the birds that have no use for song
passed over me
like a shovel-fall."

She closed her eyes. It was early morning. Daybreak.
Some bees
were dying on my wing—humming
so you could hardly hear.

LINOLEUM

for Mark Strand

There are the few we hear of
like Christ, who, with divine grace,
made goodness look easy, had
a following to draw near, gave up
the right things and saw to it
sinners got listened to.
Sharpening my failures, I remember
the Jains, the gentle swoosh
of their brooms on a dirt path
trodden by children and goats, each
thoughtful step taken in peril of
an ant's life or a fat grub hidden
under a stick. In the car wash,
thinking of yogis under a tree
plucking hair by hair the head
of an initiate, I feel at least
elsewhere those able for holiness—
its signs and rigors—are at work.
Ignominiously, I am here, brushes
clamped, soap and water pulsing
against my car. (A good sign too,
those asylums for old and diseased
animals.) My car is clean
and no one has had to
lift a finger. The dead
bugs have been gushed away into a soup
of grit and foam—the evidence
not subterranean, but streaming along
the asphalt in sunlight so dazzling

I attend the birth-moment of
the word *Hosannah!*

I care about the bugs and not
in this life will I do enough towards
my own worth in the memory
of them. I appreciate the Jains,
their atonements for my neglect,
though I understand it makes poor farmers
of them, and good we all
don't aspire to such purity so
there's somebody heartless enough to
plow the spuds.

Early on, in admiration, I put off
knowledge, and so delayed reading about
the Jains—not to lose
solace. But in the county library,
turning a page, I meet them as
the wealthiest moneylenders
in Western India. Reading on,
I'm encouraged—the list of virtues
exceeds vices—just four
of those: anger, pride, illusion and
greed. The emphasis clearly on
striving. I write them down
in the corner of a map
of Idaho: forbearance, indulgence,
straightforwardness, purity,
veracity, restraint, freedom from
attachment to anything, poverty
and chastity.

Choosing, getting into the car to
get to the supermarket, hearing
over engine noise the bright agonies
of birds, the radio news with the child
nailed into a broom closet for
twenty-four hours by parents who
in straightforwardness sacrificed
forbearance, I feel a longing
for religion, for doctrine swift
as a broom to keep the path
clear. Later, alone in the kitchen
with the groceries, I read the list
again. Overwhelmed by the loneliness
of the saints, I take up my broom
and begin where I stand,
with linoleum.

Each Bird Walking

Not while, but long after he had told me,
I thought of him, washing his mother, his
bending over the bed and taking back
the covers. There was a basin of water
and he dipped a washrag in and
out of the basin, the rag
dripping a little onto the sheet as he
turned from the bedside to the nightstand
and back, there being no place

on her body he shouldn't touch because
he had to and she helped him, moving
the little she could, lifting so he could
wipe under her arms, a dipping motion
in the hollow. Then working up from
the feet, around the ankles, over the
knees. And this last, opening
her thighs and running the rag firmly
and with the cleaning thought
up through her crotch, between the lips,
over the V of thin hairs—

as though he were a mother
who had the excuse of cleaning to touch
with love and indifference
the secret parts of her child, to graze
the sleepy sexlessness in its waiting
to find out what to do for the sake
of the body, for the sake of what only
the body can do for itself.

So his hand, softly at the place
of his birth-light. And she, eyes deepened
and closed in the dim room.
And because he told me her death as
important to his being with her,
I could love him another way. Not
of the body alone, or of its making,
but carried in the white spires of trembling
until what spirit, what breath we were
was shaken from us. Small then,
the word *holy*.

He turned her on her stomach
and washed the blades of her shoulders, the
small of her back. "That's good," she said,
"that's enough."

On our lips that morning, the tart juice
of the mothers, so strong in remembrance, no
asking, no giving, and what you said, this
being the end of our loving, so as not to hurt
the closer one to you, made me look
to see what was left of us
with our sex taken away. "Tell me," I said,
"something I can't forget." Then the story of
your mother, and when you finished,
I said, "That's good, that's enough."

BIRD-WINDOW-FLYING

If we had been given names to love
each other by, I would take this one
from you, bird flying all day
in my woodhouse. The door
is open as when you came
to it, into it, as space between branches. "Never
trust doors," you tell the window,
the small of your body flung
against the white bay.

At dusk when I walked in
with my armload of green alder,
I could see the memory of light
shining water through your wings. You
were gray with it. The window
had aged you with promises.
I thought the boats, the gulls
should have stilled you
by now. When I cupped

my hands in their shadows, warm
over the heartwings, I saw the skin
of light between my fingers
haloed and glowing. Three steps I
took with you, for
you, three light years traveling
to your sky, beak
and claw of you, the soft burr of flight
at my fingerbones.

If I take a lover for every tree, I
will not have again such an opening as
when you flew from me.
I have gone in to build my fire. All
the walls, all the
wings of my house are burning. The flames
of me, the long hair
unbraiding.

from

Amplitude

1987

"*Words lead to deeds. . . . They prepare the soul,
    make it ready
and move it to tenderness.*"

SAINT TERESA

*What sort of times are these?
And who has a clear conscience?*

*Eat, drink and be thankful!—
But how can I do this
If my food belongs
To the starving
My drink to the parched?*

At the same time, I eat and drink.

DEREK MAHON
"BRECHT IN SVENDBORG"

REFUSING SILENCE

Heartbeat trembling
your kingdom
of leaves
near the ceremony
of water, I never
insisted on you. I admit
I delayed. I was the Empress
of Delay. But it can't be
put off now. On the sacred branch
of my only voice—I insist.
Insist for us all,
which is the job
of the voice, and especially
of the poet. Else
what am I for, what use
am I if I don't
insist?
There are messages to send.
Gatherings and songs.
Because we need
to insist. Else what are we
for? What use
are we?

If Poetry Were Not a Morality

*It is likely I would not have devoted
myself to poetry in this world which remains
insensitive to it, if poetry were not a morality.*

JEAN COCTEAU
PAST TENSE

I'm the kind of woman who
when she hears Bobby McFerrin sing without words
for the first time on the car radio has to
pull over and park with the motor
running. And Cecil Taylor, I pulled over
for him too, even though later the guy
at the record store said he was just
a 'side man.' Something he did with silence and
mixing classical with I'm-worried-about-this-but-I-
have-to-go-this-way-anyhow. *This* not letting me
go. What did you do, the guy asked me, when you
pulled over? Smiled, I said, sat

and smiled. If the heart could be that simple. The photo
of Gandhi's last effects taped near
my typewriter: eyeglasses, sandals, writing paper
and pen, low lap-sized writing desk and something
white in the foreground like a bedroll.
Every so often I glance at this, just paper torn
from a book, and wish I could get down to
that, a few essentials, no
more. So when I left this place it would be
humbly, as in those welfare funerals my mother
used to scorn because the county always bought

the cheapest coffins, no satin lining, and if you
wanted the dead to look comfortable
you had to supply your own
pillow. I still admire her hating to see the living
come off cheap in their homage to any life. She
was Indian enough so the kids used to
taunt me home with "Your mother's a squaw!"
Cherokee, she said. And though nobody
told me, I knew her grandfather had to be
one of those chiefs who could never

get enough horses. Who if he had two hundred
wanted a hundred more and a hundred more
after that. Maybe he'd get up in the night and go
out among them, or watch their grazing
from a distance under moonlight. He'd pass his mind
over them where they pushed their muzzles into
each other's flanks and necks and their horseness
gleamed back at him like soundless music until
he knew something he couldn't know
as only himself, something not to be told again
even by writing down the doing

of it. I meet him like that sometimes,
wordless and perfect, with more horses than he
can ride or trade or even know why
he has. His completeness needs to be stern, measuring
what he stands to lose. His eyes
are bronze, his heart is bronze with the mystery
of it. Yet it will change his sleep
to have gazed beyond memory, I think, without sadness or

fear onto the flowing backs of horses. I look down
and see that his feet are bare, and I
have never seen such beautiful prideless feet set
on the earth. He must know what he's doing, I think, he
must not need to forgive himself the way I do

because this bounty pours onto me
so I'm crushed by surrender, heaped and
scattered and pounded into the dust with wanting more,
wanting feet like that to drive back
the shame that wants to know why
I have to go through the world like an overwrought
magnet, like the greedy braille of so many
about-to-be-lost memories. Why I can't just
settle down by the side of the road and turn the music
up on one of those raw uncoffined voices of
the dead—Bob Marley, Billie Holiday or the way Piaf
sang "Non, Je Ne Regrette Rien"—so that when

the purled horse in the music asks what I want with it
we are swept aside by there being no answer except
not to be dead to each other, except for those few
moments to belong beyond deserving to
that sumptuousness of presence, so the heart
stays simple like the morality of
a robin, the weight of living so clear a mandate
it includes everything about this junkshop
of a life. And even some of our soon-to-be deadness
catches up to us
as joy, as more horses than we need.

WITH STARS

My mother speaks from the dark—why
haven't I closed my eyes? Why don't I
sleep? And when I say I can't, she
wraps the quilt around me and leads me
to the window. I am four years old and
a star has the power of wishes.
We stare out together, but she sees past
their fierce shimmering sameness, each
point of light the emblem
of some lost, remembered face. What
do they want? I ask. "Not to be
forgotten," she says, and draws me close.
Then her gaze sifts the scattered brilliance.
Her hand goes out—"There! that one!" so
her own mother, dead years back, looks down
on us. Sleep then like a hammer
among the orbiting dead.

Tonight it is the stars reminding
keeps me up past midnight.
My mother's voice, as in that childhood room,
is with me so surely I might rush out
and find that window, those stars
no further than the next doorway, and her
there waiting—awake all night
because I was awake. "Go
to sleep," I'd say. "They want me
awake tonight." And she'd know who I meant—
those others still living and afar
because I think them there. And why not
give the dead this benefit of separations?

There were so many nameless before.
But oh, if one falls, *if*—
how can that child ever fall asleep
until sunrise?

His Shining Helmet; Its Horsehair Crest

I was reading the novel
about a war fought on horseback, reading
with the pleasure of a child given horror as
splendor. The moment came when
the soldier rose in his saddle and
the rim of the saddle was shorn
away. There the story broke off.
Then the survey of fallen comrades and
the field trampled around those with
"wounds to the head and breast." Strange
how I thought of the horses during
these tinted portraits, the horses, mentioned
only as "he rode," "his mount
stumbled," or "he bent from
the saddle to retrieve the standard, then
galloped on."

I close the book and see then
the one they did not speak of—the one
wounded in the face, the one
with his hand caught in the mane of
his horse, which lies beside and
over him, its eyes still open and its breath
a soft plunging to which the novelist
would add a "light rain" or
"a distant thunder of cannons."

But in the closed book, this
is the long moment I look into—the future
in which the wounds, as they say in the manual,
will be "non-specific, though

fatal." How far
from the single admonition of the Hittite cavalry
to simply: "Kill
the horse."

All Day the Light Is Clear

Today I wished without mercy
in the bloodless nations of the mind
that a city had gone down with you
as in a war fought—not
on foreign soil, but here
in the part of the country I can't
do without. Then, if I wept for you
inexplicably, as I have
on street corners, I could say the name
of that city and ignite in the memories
of strangers, a companion
sorrow. "Yes," they would say, "Yes,
we know," giving again that name
like a fountain
in some dusty village where the women pause,
dash water across their brows,
and pass on.

And though I shame such power and force it
from my mind, you enter this street
as a touch on the shoulder, a stare that
speaks, or in the brief nods
between workers at change of shift.
I lean on their conquering faces.
I add you to the heap, to the beautiful
multitude for whom only singing
and silence may serve—those
of our city, city of the unmiraculous,
undiminished belonging, toward which
in the green fields—as did the women
of Leningrad—I bow, bow again
and make no sound.

PHOTOGRAPH OF A LIGHTHOUSE THROUGH FOG

I said: dark voyage, I am deeply wounded
    and desire still in me
        like an eel.
I said: shards and trembling.
Said: the golden light of the sea.
Said: I cannot separate your light from
        your silence.

This reaches him like a photograph
of the lighthouse on a clear day. What is it
    for? this disabled
          windmill, this moon
      in armor?

      The rest without cunning or blame.
        Fog
rolls in with its 'vale of the soul,' its
    fledgling obedience, daring to ask:
        where are we now?
        Caught in some ruby-throated
pain; its staple of hope
        mercenary as the word
      eternity.

I said: vigil and a body that dies.
I said: heart not of this shore, the birds fly
        through me.
Said: I once lived dark
      like honey, deepest in
        pleasure after the pleasure.

Said: halo, memory dampens my
                memory. I can't know
                                how far I shine.

Pain, he said, is advice I never take. Any cat
knows what to do in the aviary.

The photographer lashes the camera to his arm,
                hoping to record light as
                        inscription, its
                                baptismal slapping
        against water.
                But is
        that salty staccato warning or invitation?

                        Stay away, I said. *Stay*
                        away.

PRESENT

She could hold me with stories, those
of people whose names and doings
were a fluttering at the brain, scattered
or wafted in the current of her voice, softly
away. Those lives happened out of her
and into me and out again, because I couldn't
remember, only be warmed by them. Somehow
my forgetting insured returns to that hovering
population in her memory, of which,
as I found, I was a part.

She said she thought maybe she couldn't have
children, maybe nothing would come. She
and my father together by then two years.
His being dead now, not coming into this, but
there too, as if he couldn't hear us,
but we could know for him. "I'd go up into
the woods where he was logging, do what I could,
work hard as two men myself. That day

on Round Mountain your dad and his partner
got ahead of me. I'd been working.
I hadn't seen where I was. Suddenly I was
alone, walking this old logging road, fireweed
over my head. I stood still and listened
to the birds and other sounds—wind and
little fallings and shiftings in the undergrowth,
animal stirrings. *It's so beautiful
here!* I kept thinking. *I've never been anywhere
so beautiful!* I was alone with the mountain. Sun

shattering down through the trees onto ferns
and fallen logs. It's peaceful here, I thought.
Then it came to me, like the mountain had told
me, and I knew it was over. One waiting was
over. And another was starting. The feeling so
sure I put my hands on my belly and pressed
a little against where the carrying had started
before I'd known it. Knowing then, so you'd
stopped happening without me. We, I thought,
We. And I thought of your father not

knowing yet, and it seemed you were knowing for
him already, were rushing ahead of me like
an action I had no part in, but was all of me
and some of him that I was about to let you tell
him. Isn't that what conception is? Agreeing
to take the consequences of things so far
beyond you that a trembling takes over and more
is shaken out of us than we can
possibly account for?" And something else, she
said, the elevation of mountains, the way

beauty makes things want to join
each other. Then far off, like an echo of
itself, the *swish-swish* of the crosscut,
the steady rhythm of the blade limber against
a tree. She started to walk, still thinking how
beautiful it was all around her, the partnership
of the saw blade raking through the silence
as she made her way toward the far away
splintering, the rending of the heartwood she
knew would fall, would crash down, shuddering

the length of itself against the trees still
standing, while like a deer, picking its way
through underbrush to the edge of
the clearing, she moved, until
they saw her back into human shape. A woman
whose whereabouts they had wondered vaguely
about as they worked. And as she joined them,
they kept on with their working.

Cougar Meat

Carried this morning in the dodge and swoop
of error, rethinking a breach
with a friend—how I'd failed to staunch harm
with kindness when she needed me
as sacrifice—then you, brother, came in
to say goodbye, hovered in my kitchen
for coffee. You'd been hunting cougar three days
and nights, with your dogs, somewhere
in the mountains back of Gardiner. You hadn't
slept, keeping the fever up until the magic
gave in to you. But on the third day
snow, the invisible current of pursuit
exchanged for tracks. The kill then, baffling
and simple—awesome death made perfunctory
with a shot. I hear you out, know why

you've come, certain of welcome, yet your act
hated for the usual "female" reasons, or so
you think, and are freed of wonder and of
shame. Should I ask, Pharaoh, did you eat
of the heart? Did you find it sweet? Or,
in a bounty of silence, know the pelt
torn away, the carcass unquenchable where it fell
in its blue efficiency, its avalanche of
unmeaning which allows those man-sized footsteps
to point away unknown, yet deeply familiar. Mine
to ask whose wildness we are, whose trust
soon to be plundered? The adrenalin has let you
down. You're bone-weary and back with
the rest of us, diamond bright with hunger,

unfulfilled by the dominant courage here toward
livelihood with all its unedifying hazards.
Should I put aside kinship with the hunted and
the dumb, pray that cougars last for men like you?
Only in the mind's rarified traffic with the sacred
have I met cougar. Could have gone all day, all
life not thinking *cougar*, had you kept
from here. Wild Horse Annie, in that same untutored
leap, defended mustangs in the Pryor Mountains,
never having laid eyes on one. Enough to guess
spirits of the West surviving in those rugged bands
pursued by helicopters. Her fear—the unseen loss,
more heritage in a Medicine Hat Pinto than
in the frontier mandate to take what

you can. "Good eating too," you say, still
talking cougar. "The word is, it tastes like pork
or veal, not that I'd know." You launch into story:
"That time Dad forgot his lunch and one of the guys
on the dock offered him a sandwich, which he
ate. At poker break, he said to the guy, 'What
kind of sandwich was that, anyway?'
'Me-ow!' the guy said, and he didn't mean pussycat.
Dad looked at him, said 'It's better than snake,
by God, better than flying squirrel, and I've
eat both with appetite to spare.' Cougar meat!" my
brother says, like somebody has handed him a bat
on a skewer. *Not nature, but the visions she*

gave me, Rilke said. I kiss your cheek, brother,
where we stand on the porch. You're off

on your first vacation to an exotic place—Hawaii,
paradise regained, where you will lie down with
the lamb. You tell me you want your son brought up
to hunt cougar. If you die tomorrow in a plane crash,
I'm supposed to see to that. Don't
count on it, I say. Not one iota have I moved you,
but all day I wear dread in your name, and in the name
of Cougar, renewing in heart the biblical sacrifice of
Uzzah, whose unthinking touch on the Ark of the Covenant
was death to him, instruction for us. Recovering
that clear shot in the snow, these intricacies
of undoing, for which language was also given
to say: the meat was not wasted.

The Hands of the Blindman

In the square room
without windows
where the hours fill our pockets
with soft money, you reach
for simple things: the circle
of ash, the cup, its warm
liquid eye, the telephone, its knowing
that voices are always blind.

Walking from work, you wave fire
past your cigarette. There
is the hand of the stranger, now
the muzzles of dogs, the
rain. Touching my face once, you
were the rain, the stranger—
yet never did anyone in the dark
leave hands on me as you.

RIJL

To be a child named after a star
is to be given earth and heaven too, never
to find the dark unpossessive where you stand,
enraptured to the ground. Foot
of the Giant, Rijl al Musalsalah—Foot of the Woman
in Arabic, Heaven's Great General to
the Chinese who invented lotus feet for their women—
not just the foot miniaturized, but folded so
the underside of heel and
toes press together to blunt each step with
helplessness. Such a walker

I saw once near the Forbidden Palace
in Beijing, accompanied by her granddaughter.
Their hobbled steps still fresh to the mind that knows
there were poets who praised this exchange of pain
for beauty. I stumble among these duller earth-stars
to hang giants of another kind, so that from your sky
overflowing with immortals, you will look down
as we look up, to feel distance as kinship, splendor
as the white heads of our mothers. Algebar,
who must step as the giant bids, even

into the sea, though empowered
to survive there. Read in the legend
his interlude of blindness, how he wept on the shore—
Orion-the-hunter, the cannibal god-giant of Egypt
inscribed on the tombs as Sahu, a man running
with his head turned over his shoulder, "fleet
of foot, wide of step." And what is blindness but
the head upended in the foot so the body is all temple

or none? Intention, that willful god
of the strong, can't send a swallow from clocktower to

clothesline, yet you, child, sweep up the room, and
dancing with your arms over your head, command
to be joined, for yours is a double star, white-hot
and tinged with blue. I am your giant,
delivered to sight, going heart-in-heart
where you lead. Rai al Jauzah, herdsman of the stars,
it is winter where I write, and you are gleaming
above the hemlock, talisman
of a guardian joy. Not to you, but to the real girl
I turn, recalling a night when, dashing
from the house, she refused her sweater, calling back
for us all, "Don't you know I'm
a star? Don't you know
                    I'm burning up?"

BONFIRE

for Ray

The inflections of joy. The inflections of
                    suffering. And strangely
          sometimes the mixing
                    of the two.
It reminds me of opening the huge *International*
          Butterfly Book with over 2,000 species
                    illustrated in color
          and among them, the giant birdwing butterfly
                    Ornithoptera victoriae
obtained when John McGillivray, aboard the *HMS*
                              Rattlesnake
          used a shotgun to bring it down
                    somewhere in the Pacific.
Other wild petals shattered by use of
                    pronged arrows
                              in New Guinea.
And the laughable "mechanical butterfly" intended
          as a decoy, said to be "very successful" in
                    capturing the flashing
                              blue Morpho.

So many kinds of crying. So much raw gaiety,
          variegated with glittering
                              silence. And you,
                    my sudden bouquet,
who came to me awkwardly at the head of the stairwell
                    outside the room that sheltered
                    for so many nights
          our sleeping and loving.

To weep there
                        together
with my death all handsomely in view,
                        all open before us
            as the sea at night.
                        All tenderly
            wild in that calm.

Safe midnight, your arms strong to hold my face into
                        yours
            while the miracle of living raked
            its silky rapier down our backs.
The last time I kissed a man in fear
            my first love went to war.
But I kissed you anyway—that seal of life, letter
                        sent and received
                                    in an instant.

Once in Quebec I drank cognac in the snow and
                                    on a dare
            ice skated with my
                        friend's violin.
I'd been falling all day, diving into flesh
                        like a spirit half
            in, half out
                        of the world.
But give me a perishable, fragile beauty
            that belongs to someone else and I skate
                        like music, like
                        the wizard of
                                    the hopeful.

How many times I saved myself on behalf of
        that borrowed, that shuddering
                violin!
When I handed it back he played his bonfire
            of thanksgiving. Played
        a mazurka, then a jig, then
                            something vast
                    and aching
as when love must go on and at the same time
                            perish.

I'm talking about memory now, that moment
        in which the doctor's news
                flushed us through with dread,
                    and I hadn't swerved
            back yet
into life. Even then I didn't forget you, violin
    who threw yourself into my arms,
            violin asking not to
be broken one more time.
        It wasn't for music
                you came to me, but
                    for daring—mine
                and yours.
When they have to, they will write in the Book
        of Welcome:
                    Two darings, two darlings.

from

Moon Crossing Bridge

1992

For Ray

The world is gone,
I must carry you.

PAUL CELAN

YES

Now we are like that flat cone of sand
in the garden of the Silver Pavilion in Kyōto
designed to appear only in moonlight.

Do you want me to mourn?
Do you want me to wear black?

Or like moonlight on whitest sand
to use your dark, to gleam, to shimmer?

I gleam.   I mourn.

RED POPPY

That linkage of warnings sent a tremor through June
as if to prepare October in the hardest apples.
One week in late July we held hands
through the bars of his hospital bed. Our sleep
made a canopy over us and it seemed I heard
its durable roaring in the companion sleep
of what must have been our Bedouin god, and now
when the poppy lets go I know it is to lay bare
his thickly seeded black coach
at the pinnacle of dying.

My shaggy ponies heard the shallow snapping of silk
but grazed on down the hillside, their prayer flags
tearing at the void—what we
stared into, its cool flux
of blue and white. How just shaking at flies
they sprinkled the air with the soft unconscious praise
of bells braided into their manes. My life

simplified to "for him" and his thinned like an injection
wearing off so the real gave way to
the more-than-real, each moment's carmine
abundance, furl of reddest petals
lifted from the stalk and no hint of the black
hussar's hat at the center. By then his breathing stopped
so gradually I had to brush lips to know
an ending. Tasting then that plush of scarlet
which is the last of warmth, kissless kiss
he would have given. Mine to extend a lover's right past its radius,
to give and also most needfully, my gallant hussar,
to bend and take.

WAKE

Three nights you lay in our house.
Three nights in the chill of the body.
Did I want to prove how surely
I'd been left behind? In the room's great dark
I climbed up beside you onto our high bed, bed
we'd loved in and slept in, married
and unmarried.

There was a halo of cold around you
as if the body's messages carry farther
in death, my own warmth taking on the silver-white
of a voice sent unbroken across snow just to hear
itself in its clarity of calling. We were dead
a little while together then, serene
and afloat on the strange broad canopy
of the abandoned world.

CORPSE CRADLE

Nothing hurts her like the extravagance
of questions, because to ask is
to come near, to be humbled at the clotted nucleus.
One persistent cry bruises her cheekbones and she lets
it, lets the open chapel of her childhood brighten over
her with tree-light. Gray-white future
of alder, hypnosis of cedar as when
too much scent-of-nectar combs
her breathing. Rain on rain
like an upsurge in his sudden need to graze her
memory, bareheaded at the quayside
where he dreamily smoked a cigarette and guided her,
the satin shell of her stillness, toward
that same whiteness at the top of rain, swollen
and gradual. How lucid she is,
blurred edgeless, like listening
to be more wide awake, that music she pressed into him
in order to fascinate what beautifully
he had begun. All bird and no recall, she
thinks, and lives in his birdness, no burden
but strange lightness so she wants to be up at dawn,
the mountains fogged with snow, a world
that sleeps as if it were
all the world and, being so, able to be seen
at its beginning, freshly
given as sleep is, bleak fertility of sleep when
she thinks far into his last resting
wherein she drifted, drifts, slow and white,
deeply asking, deep with its dark below.

READING THE WATERFALL

Those pages he turned down in peaks
at the corners are kerchiefs now, tied
to the last light of each favorite tree
where he paused, marking my path
as surely as if he'd ordered squads
of birds to rustle leaves overhead.

And I do look up often, musing into
his warmed-over nests or letting
a thrum of recognition pulsate *koto*-like
as if his head were over my shoulder
in a cool fog allowed to think its way
down a marble staircase shorn
of its footfalls. In a child's crude
pea-pod canoe my amber beads float seaward
like a cargo meant to be lost.

How often I am held alive by half-a-matchstick,
remembering his voice across rooms
and going when called to hear some line
of poetry read aloud in our two-minded way
like adding a wing for ballast and
discovering flight.

So much of love is curved there
where his pen bracketed
the couplet mid-page, that my unused
trousseau seems to beckon deeply
like a forehead pressed into paradox
by too much invitation.

He lets me dress hurriedly for the journey
as a way to better leave me what vanishes
according to its readiness, as he is ready and glides now
into my long bedside Sunday
until we are like the dead pouring water
for the dead, unaware that our slender thirst
is unquenchable.

TRACE, IN UNISON

Terrible, the rain. All night, rain
that I love. So the weight of his leg
falls again like a huge tender wing
across my hipbone. Its continuing—the rain,
as he does not. Except as that caress
most inhabited. Ellipsis of
eucalyptus. His arms, his beautiful
careless breathing. Inscription
contralto where his lips graze
the bow of my neck. Muslin half-light.
Musk of kerosene in the hall, fixative
to ceaselessly this rain, in which
there is nothing to do but be happy, be
free, as if someone sadly accused
came in with their coat soaked through
and said, "But I only wanted
to weep and love," and we rolled toward
the voice like one body and said
with our eyes closed, "Then weep, then
love." Buds of jasmine threaded through
her hair so they opened after dark,
brightening the room. That morning
rain as it would fall, still
falling, and where we had lain,
an arctic light steady
in the mind's releasing.

BLACK PUDDING

Even then I knew it was the old unanswerable form of beauty
as pain, like coming onto a pair of herons
near the river mouth at dawn. Beauty as when the body
is a dumb stick before the moment—yet goes on,
gazes until memory prepares a quick untidy room
with unpredictable visiting hours.
So I brought you there, you who didn't belong, thinking to
    outsave
memory by tearing the sacred from

its alcove. I let you see us, arms helplessly tender,
holding each other all night on that awkward couch
because our life was ending. Again and again
retelling our love between gusts of weeping.
Did I let you overhear those gray-blue dyings?
Or as I think now, like a Mongol tribesman did I stop the horse
on its desert march, take the meal of blood

from its bowed neck to be heated. This then is my black pudding
only the stalwart know to eat. How I climbed
like a damp child waking from nightmare to find
the parents intimate and still awake.
And with natural animal gladness, rubbed my face
into the scald of their cheeks, tasting salt
of the unsayable—but, like a rescuer who comes too late, too
fervently marked with duty, was unable to fathom

what their danger and passage had been for. Except
as you know now, to glimpse is intrusion enough,
and when there is nothing else to sustain, blood will be thickened
with fire. Not a pretty dish.

But something taken from the good and cherished beast
    on loan to us,
muscled over in spirit and strong enough to carry us
as far as it can, there being advantage
to this meagerness, unsavoriness that rations itself
and reminds us to respect even its bitter portion.
Don't ask me now why I'm walking my horse.

Now That I Am Never Alone

In the bath I look up and see the brown moth
pressed like a pair of unpredictable lips
against the white wall. I heat up
the water, running as much hot in as I can stand.
These handfuls over my shoulder—how once
he pulled my head against his thigh and dipped
a rivulet down my neck of coldest water from the spring
we were drinking from. Beautiful mischief
that stills a moment so I can never look
back. Only now, brightest now, and the water
never hot enough to drive that shiver out.

But I remember solitude—no other
presence and each thing what it was. Not this raw
fluttering I make of you as you have made of me
your watch-fire, your killing light.

SOUVENIR

It is good to be unused, whole as discovery—
the alabaster egg with its giant stirring.
At first, with the heat gone out of me
I thought his moon-life had lifted everything
from reach, even roses, those vermilion climbers
that were a shout at hope, up and up
my haggard trellis. But goodness
has so many silent children whose spell
lifts anchors to vessels of rock and azure, and we
go happily under our black mantle
with a tingling inside as those who live close
to the weather delight in the plain grammar
of ice, of wind over fresh tracks
through the empty valley.

So she put on her birdskin moccasins
and went out to possess her island, making sure
the tide was at ebb. Drawn by doves, she
went out with his sickle over her
in the paradise-field of stars. Wet stones
that loved with their whole being are legion
on her shore. How blackly they shine, singed and frenzied
with memory, their birth-sheen
holding on. She would throw them all back
to add intention like that proud mouth
who, in mourning, saved her drinking
only for fountains. Lucina she calls herself
under his crown of candles, Lucina with her wedding cake
crumbled into the sea. What has she saved? Rue
and red ribbon, a wreath made of tail feathers.

As with her, an early death has left its pagan mark
so everything turns to worship or sign
and I am never more alone
than when our twin gold rings come together
in a perfect chime, addressing us in the familiar
lost-future tense. I stroke her glistening hair
as he stroked mine, absently, the way candlelight licks
the night clean until one of us is gone
or disheveled into a second soul.

EMBERS

He was suffering from too much light
the way our afternoons recover from
morning rain by slicing the room
in half. I read to him to bring a voice
sideways, to touch him more, and join
our listening or laughter or mutual derision.
To be one and none. Sometimes a rhyme can
snuff its substance, yet release
a second lasting. To speak aloud at a grave
breaks silence so another heat
shows through. Not speaking, but the glow
of that we spoke.

Two of Anything

What silk-thin difference is there
if I stay to dream or go.

KYOKO SELDEN

That small tug, which at first seems
all on its own in the strait,
can eventually be seen to pull two barges, each
twice its size, because water
understands everything and all
day says "pass, pass by." I propose
a plan and we discuss it. I'm afraid I'll never
be happy again. "Bring me
a glass of water," he says. "Someone, you know,
has to stay here and take care of things."
Two ducks fly by. I take
a few sips from his glass. Outside it's
deep blue morning, almost purple
it's so glad to be cheating
the sleepers of its willful drifting, the tangled
blue of night and the blue premonition
that will dissolve and carry
it. Two boys vicious with news fling
the morning paper house to house
down the hill. Two horses out of childhood I loved,
Daisy and Colonel Boy, are hitched
to the wagon. I hear the cold extravagance of
tiny bells welded into their harness straps.
Iron wheels under us over snow
for miles through the walnut groves. The two
pearled hair combs he gave me
make a chilly mouth on the sill. I look up and out

over water at the horizon—no, two
horizons. One reached and entered with him, and so
is under me, and the other
far enough away to be the dead mate of this one.
Between them, lively passage of boats, none
empty. That's fascinating,
I said to the poet, let me add one. I thought
there was more water in this glass.
I guess not, one of us said.

COLD CRESCENT

Walking idly through the shops on the wharf
while waiting for the ferry to take us
across—we don't know yet
you are dying. But I hold that black shawl so long,
admiring lace against flesh, the way it enhances me cold
like bird song over snow, partial
and what we vanish from. So you were unafraid and
offered to buy it for me. And neither of us
noticed overmuch as money was paid
and into my hands it was
delivered, a simple swath of cloth.

I remember taking it freshly
out of the drawer, the crispness of black, its
breaking off at both ends into daylight, as death
breaks us off or shouts into itself
until a tingling ambushes the room and it is all we can do
not to follow that swoop of not-coming-backness.

But I'm past that now, as the crescent moon says
of its full stony profile. Tonight the moon is blond.
His sideways light bends inward to cheat
the dark. That's why he's here, to hand me
the white shawl knitted beside some missing fire.
When he sets it across my shoulders
I am lowered gently down
and made to sleep again on earth.

After the Chinese

By daybreak a north wind has shaken
the snow from the fir boughs. No disguise
lasts long. Did you think there were no winds
under the earth? My Tartar horse prefers
a north wind. Did you think
a little time and death would stop me?
Didn't you choose me for the stubborn
set of my head, for green eyes that dared
the cheat and the haggler from our door?
I've worn a little path, an egg-shaped circle
around your grave keeping warm
while I talk to you. I'm the only one
in the graveyard. You chose well. No one
is as stubborn as me, and my Tartar horse
prefers a north wind.

BLACK VALENTINE

I run the comb through his lush hair,
letting it think into my wrist
the way the wrist whispers to the cards
with punctuation and savvy in a game of solitaire.
So much not to be said the scissors
are saying in the hasp and sheer
of the morning. Eleven years I've cut
his hair and even now, this last time, we hide
fear to save pleasure
as bulwark. *My dearest*—the hair says as it brushes my
thighs—*my only*—on the way to the floor. If the hair
is a soul-sign, the soul obeys our gravity, piles up
in animal mounds and worships the feet. We're
silent so peace rays over us like Bernice's hair
shaken out across the heavens. If there were gods
we are to believe they animated her shorn locks
with more darkness than light, and harm
was put by after the Syrian campaign, and
harm was put by as you tipped the cards
from the table like a child bored
with losing. I spread my hair like a tent over us
to make safety wear its twin heads, one to face death,
the other blasted so piteously by love
you throw the lantern of the moment against
the wall and take me in with our old joke, the one
that marks my northern skies, "Hey babe," you say
like a man who knows how to live on earth. "Hey,"
with your arm around my hips, "what you doing
after work?" Silly to ask now if the hair
she put on the altar, imagining her power over
his passage, was dead or living.

FRESH STAIN

I don't know now if it was kindness—we do
and we do. But I wanted you with me
that day in the cool raspberry vines, before
I had loved anyone, when another girl and I
saw the owner's son coming to lift away
our heaped flats of berries. His
white shirt outside his jeans so
tempting. That whiteness, that quick side-glance
in our direction. We said nothing,
but quickly gathered all the berries we could, losing
some in our mirth and trampling them
like two black ponies who only want to keep their backs
free, who only want to be shaken with
the black night-in-day murmur of hemlocks
high above. Our slim waists, our buds
of breasts and red stain of raspberries cheapening
our lips. We were sudden, we were
two blurred dancers who didn't need paradise. His shirt,
his white shirt when the pelting ended, as if
we had kissed him until his own blood
opened. So we refused every plea and
were satisfied. And you didn't touch me then, just
listened to the cool silence after. Inside,
the ripe hidden berries as we took up our wicker baskets
and lost our hands past the wrists
in the trellised vines. Just girls with the arms of
their sweaters twisted across their hips, their laughter
high in sunlight and shadow, that girl
you can almost remember as she leans into the vine,
following with pure unanswerable desire, a boy
going into the house to change his shirt.

Rain-soaked Valentine

As if some child, unwilling to shut even
the figurative heart into pocket or
lunch pail, had carried it plate-like
home in a downpour. A passionate
migration—no matter its redundant shape
and thirty others just as crude. The passage
did it good, white lace bleeding, the stock
message smudged out of language by rivulets
and soaring. It came with a lunge,
earnestness of moment, refusing
to be merely "sufficient" as in prudent love—
the effect gauged before the gift.
Anciently worn to trash on its way to me, it
doesn't care if I am moonlight. Just arriving
is candor, is courting.

Meeting beyond Meeting

There is threat of you here as the sea
shows its blackest hour before nightfall,
then doubles back to take it all.
But for a while the trees are silhouetted
against a band of shaggy lavender across
a bridge of pink-edged light.
I could still believe the door will open
and you will be standing there,
a little surprised I'm not with
anyone yet.

Now the light's extinguished
and we who knew every curve and dip and scar
must claim each other like hands picking orchids
in the dark. We can tell only by the fragrance
how much needs crushing.

PARADISE

Morning and the night uncoupled.
My childhood friend
who had been staying awake for me, left the house
so I could be alone with the powerful raft of his body.

He seemed to be there only for listening, an afterlife
I hadn't expected. So I talked to him, told him
things I needed to hear myself
tell him, and he listened, I can say "peacefully,"
though maybe it was only an effect he had, the body's surety
when it becomes one muscle. Still, I believe I heard
my own voice then, as he might have heard it, eagerly
like the nostrils of any mare blowing softly over
the damp presence he was, telling it
all is safe here, all is calm and yet to be endured
where you are gone from.

I spoke until there was nothing unfinished between us.
Since his feet were still there and my hands
I rubbed them with oil
because it is hard to imagine at first
that the dead don't enjoy those same things they did
when alive. And even if it happened only as a last thing, it
was the right last thing.

For to confirm what is forever beyond speech
pulls action out of us. And if it is only childlike and
unreceived, the way a child hums to the stick
it is using to scratch houses into the dirt, still
it is a silky membrane and shining
even to the closed eye.

EBONY

I need these dark waves pulsing in my sleep.
How else make up for the pungency
of that carnation's breath freshened over us,
night on night? Just to lie next to love
was to have the garden in all its seasons.
I see that now. Gently, and without
the false luster of pain meant to tempt
memory into crushed fragrance.
In the pull and toss of stones below the house
a soothing spirit sifts and laves its weights,
and those that were tears in some oriental legend
are strongly effaced in the wearing. You,
who were only a stone, taught stone to me in aftermath.
Which is to mock containment at its rich periphery.
The gray, the green in my black.

FATHOMLESS

The peacock has eaten the poison orchid
and shakes poison into beauty of feathers as
easily as my hair unlatches its
black hairpins into the pool
the sunken grave has made of him.
They drop and drop.
From a long way off I hear them strike bone
that could be eye-socket or pelvis or
sternum. The sound is not what I
expected. Not the startled gold
of his wedding band. Not that. More
the soft plinging of arrows shot
in a dream toward my own face, stopped there,
above a pool where someone else's tears
have broken unruly, and fall softly
through the eye.

DEAF POEM

Don't read this one out loud. It isn't
to be heard, not even in the sonic zones
of the mind should it trip the word "explosion"
and detonate in the silent room. My love
needs a few words that stay out of
the mouth and vocal cords. No vibrations, please.
He needs to put his soul's freshly inhuman capacity
into scattering himself deeper into
the forest. It's part of the plan that birds
will eat the markings. It's okay. He's not coming
that way again. He likes it where he is. Or if he
doesn't, I can't know anything about it. Let
the birds sing. He always liked to hear them
any time of day. But let this poem meet
its deafness. It pays attention another way, like he
doesn't when I bow my head and press my forehead
in the swollen delusion of love's power to
manifest across distance the gladness that joined us.

Wherever he is he still knows I have two feet
and one of them is broken from dancing.
He'd come to me if he could. It's nice to be sure
of something when speaking of the dead. Sometimes
I forget what I'm doing and call out to him. It's me! How
could you go off like that? Just as things were
getting good. I'm petulant, reminding him of his promise
to take me in a sleigh pulled by horses
with bells. He looks back in the dream—the way
a violin might glance across a room at its bow
about to be used for kindling. He doesn't
try to stop anything. Not the dancing. Not the deafness

of my poems when they arrive like a sack of wet
stones. Yes, he can step back into life just long enough
for eternity to catch hold, until one of us
is able to watch and to write the deaf poem,
a poem missing even the language
it is unwritten in.

WE'RE ALL PHARAOHS WHEN WE DIE

Our friends die with us
    and the sky too
        in huge swatches, and lakes, and places
           we walked past, just going and
              coming.
The spoons we ate with look dim, a little deadened
    in the drawer. Their trips to the mouth
        forlorn, and the breath caught there
           fogged to a pewter smudge.

Our friends die with us and are thrown in because we
used them so well.
But they also stay on earth awhile like the abandoned
    huts of the Sherpas on a mountain that doesn't know
        it's being climbed. They don't fall down all at once.
           Not like his heart
fell down, dragging
the whole gliding eternity of him out of sight.

Guttural and aslant, I chew the leather sleeve
    of his jacket, teething like a child on the unknown pressure
        budding near its tongue. But the tongue
           is thrown in too, everyone's who said his name
as he used to be called
in our waking and sleeping,
    dreaming and telling the dreams.
        Yes, the dreams are thrown in
so the mystery
    breaks through still wearing its lid, and I am never
        to be seen again
           out of his muslin striding.

If this is my lid then, with its eyebrows painted on, with its
stylized eyes glazed open above the yet-to-be-dead ones, even so
             a dead-aliveness looks through
                      as trees are thrown in
                               and clouds and the meadows under the
                                        orchards
the deer like to enter—those returning souls
         who agree to be seen
                      gazing out of their forest-eyes
with our faint world painted over them.

MOON CROSSING BRIDGE

If I stand a long time by the river
when the moon is high
don't mistake my attention
for the merely aesthetic, though
that saves in daylight.
Only what we once called worship
has feet light enough to carry
the living on that span of brightness.
And who's to say I didn't cross
just because I used the bridge in its witnessing,
to let the water stay the water
and the incongruities of the moon to chart
that joining I was certain of.

Spacious Encounter

What they cut away in braids from childhood
returns. I use it. With my body's nearest silk
I cover you in the dream-homage, attend and revive
by attending. I know very little of what to do
without you. Friends say, "Go on with your life."
But who's assigned this complicitous extension,
these word-caressings? This night-river
full of dead star-tremors, amazed floatings, our
chaotic laboratory of broken approaches.

Your unwritten pages lift an ongoing dusk in me.
Maybe this makes me your only reader now. The one
you were writing towards all along, who can't put down
her double memory pressed to shape
your one bodiless body. Book I am wearing in my night-rushing
to overtake these kneelings and contortions of daylight. Book
that would be a soul's reprisal
if souls could abandon their secret missions
so necessary to our unbelief. No,
the embrace hasn't ended.
Though everyone's grief-clock
runs down. Even mine sweeps
the room and goes forth with a blank face
more suited each day to enduring.

Ours is the compressed altitude
of two beings who share one retina
with the no-world seared onto it, and
the night-river rushing through, one-sided,
and able to carry what is one-sidedly felt
when there is no surface to what

flows into you. Embrace
I can't empty. Embrace I would know with my arms
cut away on no street in no universe
to which we address so much unprofound silence.
I unshelter you—my vanishing
dialogue, my remnant, my provision.

ANNIVERSARY

If the sun could walk into a room
you would not dare to want
such a man as he. But blindness
has prepared me, is requisite
to love put away, like breath
put away from the half-opened mouth,
breath that returns, withdraws,
returns again. As he does
and does not.

We ate the wedding feast quietly
and to ourselves near the hush
of the gaming tables, the icy click
of dice in the half-closed hand
before they are thrown.
There were no toasts to the future
because by then it was a day
about to begin, already stunted
by the hazard of its own
oblivion. What could I tell you
of love at that moment
that would be simple and true enough
since words are candles I blow out
the moment I set them down?
Better to scrape wax from the table edge
with a fingernail. Better to stare
into the eye of a horse
brought to drink from the mouth
of a river where it opens
into the sea. All was liquid
and tranquil there, and though our lips

were kept from touching
by the great sleep of space
before us, everything poured into us
hard and true, and when we set our glasses
down, the darkness of the horse's
overflowing eye closed over us.

I Stop Writing the Poem

to fold the clothes. No matter who lives
or who dies, I'm still a woman.
I'll always have plenty to do.
I bring the arms of his shirt
together. Nothing can stop
our tenderness. I'll get back
to the poem. I'll get back to being
a woman. But for now
there's a shirt, a giant shirt
in my hands, and somewhere a small girl
standing next to her mother
watching to see how it's done.

CHERRY BLOSSOMS

Chekhov wanting to write about "the wave of
child suicides sweeping across Russia"—plunged
by that sentence into sudden pity for
myself and my three brothers growing up,
as my father had, under the strap. Pity
for my father who worked and slept, worked
and drank and was the dispenser of woe.
Our child bodies learning despair, learning to quake
and cower—the raw crimson of pain given by
the loving hand. No wonder, for a while,

animals drew close to us, as if our souls
overlapped. And so we died there. And were
attended by animals. One dog especially
I remember with brightest gratitude.
Miles of night and her wild vowellings under
great moons, subsiding into a kind of atrocious
laughter, what I think of now as faint gleams
of demoniac nature ratifying itself. Somehow

that viewless dread she recorded seared
my childhood with survival—she who
was mercifully and humbly buried somewhere
with a little *sotoba* over her, bearing the unnecessary
text: "Even within such as this animal,
    the Knowledge Supreme will enfold at last."
              And so my old friend died.
And the cherry blossoms fell sumptuously.
And I wrote a little *sotoba* in my determined
         child-hand, to insure that never again
could they be put back
              onto our bare branches.

KNOTTED LETTER

*It seems to me, though, that you
always understand very well what I
can't say very well.*

HARUKI MURAKAMI
A WILD SHEEP CHASE

There is that getting worse at saying
that comes from being understood
in nuance, because the great illiteracy
of rain keeps writing over my days
as if to confirm the possibility
of touching everything so it glistens
with its bliss bent aside by some soft
undirected surpassing.

I say to the never-injured creature:
the shears have rent my silk—unsolving
beauty, hard and bright—until I am so consequent
with time it is accomplice
and spills neither backwards nor
forwards. I ask him to live by miscalculation
my capricious scheme. Counsel him to miss light
an oar's moment and be ocean-cold
as love's splashing after-touch, the blade-edge
actual, but under spell
and scarlet to what it gladly slips
as a thing too near and precious—a shadowy fish
drowsy with the overgarment of planets and stars
it haunts below, as if to commemorate
the unseen by the marbled distortions
guessed at. Because the kisses come mixed with sand

and we know the mouth is full of strange, unwieldy
sediment. And because the samurai image of a sword
is thrust through clouds with only the hilt
showing, its unglinting edges like words
slashed to stubble where the wheat was gathered.

And this a gleaning twisted to the leafless bush
he was sure to pass, thinking by memory
her waist-length hair, her spoken face
as he would never see it, in the words
of poems so keenly obscured
the poem was her only face.

PICKING BONES

Emiko here from Tokyo in her red dress
and voice like a porcelain hand
on silk. We carry roses to the grave
under the tilt of gulls. Some have
walked their hieroglyphics across the poem
carved there, to make sure we comprehend
this stopping off to flight. Small tasks

prepare another silence, kinship of pouring
water, fallen petals brushed across granite.
Gradually we come there after we've
come there. Hard to light candles
in the breeze from the strait. His delight
flickers and gusts. We are steady
and erased a little more. Finally we talk quietly,

the presence palpable as we crouch there.
That overlay too of new sound Emiko has given
his poems in Japanese. Our voices nudge closer
on the cliffside. Pungency and sweetness
of joss sticks, Emiko says, in Japanese cemeteries,
and smoke curling up. After cremation of the loved one,
working in pairs, the relatives join in the ritual

of "picking bones." Two by two with chopsticks lifting
each bone from the ashes, dropping it
into an urn. Her friend, Yoshi, who said he had
much feeling and grief on viewing
his father's body, but who saw and felt,
in lifting shards of a father—the lightness, the necessary
discrepancy of translation. For a moment we are held

precariously as a morsel
on the way to any mouth. "Don't
pick bones!" the mothers warn children caught
lifting the same piece of food. We pull
ourselves up from the low black table, from

                                the ivory clicking.

At the-Place-of-Sadness

I take a photo of the stone Buddha
gazing from its eternal moment over
the eroded bodies of hundreds of child-sized
Buddhas. Shoulder to shoulder
they say something about death
not to be offered another way. The spirits
of those with no relatives to mourn them, an entity
driving tears inward so the face wears only the gust,
the implosion of grief.

Through the starred red of maple leaves: a man
half-visible in white shirt and black tie
held on a level with the stone Buddha—the one
in its living stillness, the other more-than-living
so he takes a step toward me
when I press the shutter
and glance up
like one of the dead
given the task of proving, with two identical stones,
the difference between
a spirit and a body.

INFINITE ROOM

Having lost future with him
I'm fit now to love those
who offer no future when future
is the heart's way of throwing itself away
in time. He gave me all, even
the last marbled instant, and not as excess,
but as if a closed intention were itself
a spring by the roadside
I could put my lips to and be quenched
remembering. So love in a room now
can too easily make me lost
like a child having to hurry home
in darkness, afraid the house
will be empty. Or just afraid.

Tell me again how this is only
for as long as it lasts. I want to be
fragile and true as one who extends
the moment with its death intact,
with her too wise heart
cleansed of that debris we called hope.
Only then can I revisit that last surviving
and know with the wild exactness
of a shattered window what he meant
with all time gone
when he said, "I love you."

Now offer me again
what you thought was nothing.

GLOW

Those Japanese women waiting, waiting
all the way back to Shikibu and Komachi
for men who, even then, seemed capable
of scant affection. Traitorous though,
not to admire the love of women
that shines down long corridors of the past
as steadily as those lanterns
I walked under beside the shrines of Kyōto.
Women who waited in vain, or to have sorrow
freshened by a cursory reappearance.
Their hope of meeting even a poor love again
gave each heart its rigorous vanishing.

Even a beautiful waste is waste.
Someone should have stepped through
the cobwebs in their pitiful doorways
with a new message: "Not the work of love
but love itself, nothing less."
That at least might have emptied
them sufficiently
to carry expectation past
its false chance at fulfillment.
Which is to say—when no right love came
they would not have been ready.
Something close at hand
would have claimed their attentions.

So I walked out one night under the full moon
and agreed with my dead love
that the cold light on the backs of my hands
belonged most to me.

Un Extraño

Light begins. Snow begins.
A rose begins to unhinge
its petals. Sleep
begins. An apple lets go
of its branch. Someone tells
a secret like an echo
wrapped around a shadow,
a shadow soaked in love.
The secret begins to make
a difference. It travels
on the borrowed heat
of what the shadow
passes over. The lip
begins its mustache.
The heart begins its
savage journey
toward love and loss
of love. But you, you
don't begin. I stare
at your hand on my breast.
Their dialogue is the wingless
strength of the stem
bearing its flower
in rain, in sun.

Day begins. Night begins.
But you don't begin.
You know that one thing
the loveless lovers forget,
that to begin is to agree
to live among half-forces,

to shine only when the moon
shines and all is ready.

You make me ready
but you do not begin.
I let you never begin.
It's my gift to our most uncertain
always. I agree only to coincide
outside each death-enchanted
wave. What we are making
isn't a shroud or a halo.
It's a banished hive
stinging itself alive with
vast multiplications. We taunt love
as the bullfighter taunts
death, preparing the dangerous lunge
until it catches us unawares
that split second
in which love shudders
its starkest glimpse
into us. The magenta cape
swirls its silk across our lips
like a breath unraveled in the moment
the matador kneels to the bull.
My *adorno, el novillito*. Don't
begin. Don't ever begin.

I Don't Know You

And you don't know me.
Out of this the loudest appeal
to harm or advantage.
Don't move. I like this ledge
of loose diamonds waiting to be spilled
into the night. Let's shine awhile
without touching. Sensuality is,
after all, a river that is always waiting.
Let's wait another way. Not for
anything, but because waiting
isn't a part of nature. I don't want
to take a step toward death
in anyone's company, not even
for love's sake.

I like how you know not to speak.
If I could arrange a true moment
to startle us into a right communion,
I would have a small boy come toward us now
with a bowl of rainwater.
It isn't for us. We're as unmysterious
to him as rain falling into
rainwater. He puts his lips to the rim
and drinks, but not without seeing us.

So history is made of unconscious glances
threaded by the unreapable memories
of children. But stay a little longer
unconfessed to me as a kiss
we agree to forswear. I love
this slow carriage, the heavy bellies

of the horses, the harness which
has scraped me down to hide.

And now I know you less
and you will never know me
as one reduced by the casual
or even the half-closed eyelid of desire.
That way is ancient but, like twilight, a sign
of elements overlapped against their wills.

Ours is another luster,
as if a soul had died outside the world
and divided itself in two
in order to prepare the lucid, intricate pleasure
of its welcome.

Yes, let's agree also
not to believe in the soul.

WHILE I SIT IN A SUNNY PLACE

Tame love that remembers a birthday
but scorns the every-moment,
how you robbed the pit from the cherry,
that wooden pearl I was carrying
under my tongue. Talisman
of silence wedged between the poet's words
when I say, "Don't you know
I'm the joyful girl inside
the woman with the forever-melting ghost
on her lips?" If the word "happy"
has a future it's mine because
I don't exist in the favored shell
of what I'm meagerly given. Isn't
there enough sky? Isn't there
laughter and running? Can't the ardor
of one smiling face make a deer leap,
even when to leap could mean
an alternate calamity?

I have only these hot-cold widow's hands
to touch the world back with.
You know that and it doesn't stop you.
Something sacred, a vast accord between
my ghosted-love and how it could
convey the shadow-selves of some happiest
surrender—was this
what brought you?

Be equal to it then, like a deer that chooses
to leap over a rose. Like a rose with its leaping
above it.

The Forest She Was Trying to Say

*Tonight I feel compassion for everyone,
those who are pitied, along with those who
are kissed.*

MARINA TSVETAYEVA

The angel wings of the hemlock
aren't for flying. They are the fragrant arms
of a stately spirit held in the shape
of an unlived moment when the world,
in all its woe and splendor, disappeared.
To visit the sunless core
of the forest is to say to the heart,
which is always a remnant, "Love as if
you will be answered," and in that fiction
to force love wide
as the invisible net of bird flight
between the boughs. Here tenderness
has squeezed light to infusion.
Why is love so vengeful and absent
because one diamond kiss
fell out of his mouth with sear
intent against my throat?
Did he mean never to be thought of apart
from love? Angel, those wings
aren't for flying but in defiance
of all that harsh traffic
on the soulless plain. This
is the forest, or at least a small
forever-kneeling wood. And we are adorned
and adored here because we wear the gall
of an impossible love.

Angel, don't look at me like one
cast out and piteous. This is Eden
and the gods are elsewhere. Angel,
we will be thrown out. We will fall
down and be that other wild.

SEA INSIDE THE SEA

How well he knows he must lift out
the desolate Buddha, unfurl the scroll
raked anciently with its dragon's claw
of waiting. Silk banner embossed
with the myriad invigorations of the blood
pulling the tide toward us
until our bodies don't hoard eternity
but are spun through with a darting vehemence,
until the abundant thing made of us spikes free
of even its ripening, that moan of white fingers at a depth
that strips the gears of the soul.

I lick salt of him from under his eyes,
from the side of the face. Prise open each wave
in its rising, in its mouth-to-breast-to-groin.
A velvet motionlessness where the halo
lingers as if between two endless afternoons
in which a round presence, most quiet and
most unquiet, is tended. Because love
has decided and made a place of us.
Has once again asked its boldest question
as an answer.

We are the lucidity of salt, jealous
even of its craving. It follows
its thirst with its neck outstretched
so like the shy deer
who come down from the mountain.
They run their quick tongues
over the wet ribbons of seaweed. But we are so far inside

the body-ness of the body, that the hieroglyphics of their
    hoof prints
inscribe the many-paired lips of the sea's cave mouth
which, even now, drinks wave onto wave.

We are overspent into awakening like the pinched scent
of aniseed that carries its sex
as a bruising. He lifts himself like an answer
in which love, as it knows not to speak
but is many-chasmed, says, "Ask me. Ask me
anything." Again, his palm passes over
the mute belly, passes and repasses.
Her gold and silver rings in a heap
on the headboard. His naked hand. Hers
more naked. The sea turned back nightlong
by the blackened tide of her hair
across no shore.

Kisses from the Inside

He has invented a way of guiding
the blind woman so they can step exactly
together. As she is not led, so is he rapid
and ingenious with me. I am like a house lost
in the woods of Soto
whose upper floors are occupied by gypsies.
They braid red yarn into my hair
and light my shadow with candles to keep me
all in light. He wants me all in light,
she who was stumbling three years
with the dead. He picks my feet up
by their heels in his palm. The more
I want to be high and golden, pitiless and
unformed, the more he tears me back
to earth. He rolls me in the red dust
inside the night. Even his kisses
stroke my unwinding from the inside.
The bees fly off from their honey,
their unspeakable frenzies.
In the hovering noon of our devotional midnights
he flies off, until I am sheer and stolen,
rooted deep in the sea air
        because the tide is everything
            because the tide is everything
and I have never seen the sea.

A LIGHT THAT WORKS ITSELF INTO THE MIND

If the fish could only half-swim
like an agreement to be half-in-love
the vision of its divine fluidity might hesitate
without comfort, without being consumed. But
it must plunge in freedom-light, luminous and
natural as the language of passersby, yet imprecise
enough to keep a true identity. Light
that is a dwelling or a road that still enters
where someone has fled and forfeited a joy
from that day on. By the open window
she is braiding her hair and thinking what to give
amply, while his flesh unlives itself,
urgent at the rim of her slow unreasoning.
Where has he learned to turn back pleasure
like an almost-summer? And what does it mean,
this something lighter-than-himself
he renews in her like a letter read inside out
because its own listening asks something to be told
away from the very moment of its outward light?

Like a child's freshly kissed face
only the honest heart is free, is able
to return its dazzling to the starry, open land.
Everything he fears to tell her is like an image
that pierces the painter's canvas
from the other side. And it stays on her fingertips
as a spider-climb of heart-constraining wonder
long after his wave to wave
has worn away his mouth, the wet sacramental voice
that had been their most silent body.

Near, As All That Is Lost

Don't play it like it's love.
It's a memory of love.

What are we now, who were two unsynchronized eyelids
lifting the day-into-night world beyond its fictions
of life forever? One eye watched
the other eye in its unbound search for a way back
to a language equal to the dream-washing of our past,
that all-severed pledge each death falsely requires.

I couldn't allow the day-star behind the night-star
until another life leaped over
the beautiful rubble memory hid in me.
Now love is my joy-injured orbit like a bow
drawn by an arched wrist across two strings of a cello
and above this, the listening hand
bending one of the notes as pain-in-transit bends
language to purposes outside meaning.
Only then can it hide its resonance
in new love's shadow-drinking.

Such joining bewitches, and not through harmony,
but through a stretching of memory as we don't know
how to speak its sensations, but must play them out
as bodies, as if the wishfulness of the soul to feel
would come into us, as it comes, as it does come.

And now the shadow takes a step for
us. And I speak into the shadow
its love-name, its most tender body: *Morenito, Morenito.*

So it walks for us and lies down for us and polishes
our one body of light, the one that slides over the earth
like a black platter with the world on its shoulders,
with its feet under our feet.

Portable Kisses

¹994

Even birds help
each other. Come
close. Closer.
Help me
            kiss you.

T. G.
"LITTLE INVITATION IN A HUSHED VOICE"

WIDOW IN RED SHOES

A quiet gathering of a few old friends,
my first time with some of them
since his death. Getting ready, I think
of greeting them without him, and know
back of a momentary awkwardness,
there's an unstoppable avalanche
none of us will release. Tsvetayeva was right
in mourning Rilke—to cry is
to accept: *As long as I don't cry he hasn't*
died. Then I see them—
the red shoes, thrown into my bag
as afterthought, the spiked exclamation points
of the heels, the sharp toes out of the '6os.
They're a little worn. Not easy to replace,
a pair of shoes which went everywhere with
him. Already they have the look
of something misunderstood. I pull on
the black tights, some sort of low-waisted dress,
and slip on the shoes. He always loved
me in these red shoes. Defiant, sexy
and with him.

Kiss without a Body

You think I don't know life
humbles us to its measure?
How the magnet of beauty tears
at the skeleton, aging it
from the inside out?
Rest here a few moments, in this body
without a body that
is love, was love. These poems will
convince more than one other
you were loved greatly
and should be again. Will it be
the way a fallen star
tells the ground about the night sky?
Will she look up? that woman
in our future? But now the book
has fallen to the floor and we
have turned to each other
on the wordless stairway
of some unlived moment where poetry
means nothing, though it is all there is
of what the night would cry
if it had two voices, this one
and the one that would answer
if it could.

His Moment

They burned my bed. Took it high
and burned it, those smoldering angels
so eager to lift my one love from earth.

Now that I sleep on the ground
my bed is everywhere.
Now that I kiss the air
my love goes everywhere.

If his are the only lips,
am I never to be kissed
except as one never-to-be-kissed-again?

Sometimes the dawn sky clings
to itself like that
in the moment just after multitudes of stars
have faded. That's why I love most
the moment when you take your lips away.

LETTER TO A KISS THAT DIED FOR US

I have been writing your memoir.
It is like leaving the world
and still finding you there
as you received us, shaped us
and instantly became unrepeatable.
I keep thinking I can write a cheek against
you, if not lips. A magnetic cheek
with the taste of cold, metallic air
on it so the clang of it will stay
a little after. I tempt you with nakedness
on a terrace, with tambourines, all my gypsy
favors. With the sleek flanks of longing,
I tempt you who are gone forever,
a thought I can have
as this letter is written
outside any death.

POEMS WRITTEN ABOUT KISSES

Many real things like darkness falling
to the emptied playground or to a ship's flag
happen outside anticipation or afterthought.
But kisses on their way to us
are easily becalmed
or, once accomplished, turn back
so quickly to where they came from
we scarcely breathe out
and they are fictive
as rain which fell yesterday.
So if I write: "my lips are still wet with kisses,"
it is like photographs of fire,
the avaricious portraiture
of actions sealed imperfectly
by the gleam of memory. We must add heat
and the fear that someone may not
have gotten out alive. Consider
then the half-closed eyes
of love's pensive listening to old rain
in the mind's greedy vault. Rain
I used to know, falling onto this page
as rain yet to fall—lightly, lightly—
though kisses are torrent and torment
yesterday or tomorrow, and a poem,
like anything propelled by absent power,
eats and drinks nothing, sustains
as it consumes.

In the Laboratory of Kisses

We held our rows of lips
so far outside ourselves
a moon watching
would have known how to
unbewitch itself in water.

Gradually to shed, to be
cold silver to what might
come. And somewhere the chill
of glass on glass, the beakers
being stirred with icicles,
whir of hummingbird to add
suspension, and his lips—
so freshly long ago
against my eyelids—
I hear the lifting and
the setting down of hooves
just breaking the snow-crust.

Gentle in my black—your mare
will startle. Gentle, the noose
he makes of my glass bead necklace
looped suddenly to draw us
closer still.

Fable of a Kiss

I was lonely. Very shortly
I was lonely again.
I found myself in my mother's orchard
but she was nowhere about.
I pulled a plum
from her plum tree and took a bite.
It was bitter, mixed with
a puzzling unripeness of my own
that made me feel I had lost everything.

Birds came and went from the trees.
A brown snake slid into the iris bed.
I took a vicious bite
from the plum. It seemed to know
it had befallen my hard jaw
and participated in its violent addition.
My mouth ached: the plum flesh
shoved itself along in me
down to the shaggy pit
where loneliness changes to solitude,
and what was bitter slips
into another register, a woman's
footsteps, her kiss
on the forehead,
which for the mother
is another mouth.

Even if she is missing,
perhaps long dead, the story
of her one-time child
under a plum tree

is a kind of snare to press the lips
of the mind against, an inexact
comfort that is also a pang
and a forfeit
as the ceremony of the ever-unloved heart
unfolds, contracts, unfolds.

Kissing the Blindman

is like kissing the moon
between phases, a kind of larceny
that sweetens one light as it
quenches another. He was halls
and handsomely, a drowned lamp
in my skull, a ship in the mountain,
silk over no shoulder.

Black moon before breath,
I don't kiss you with my mouth only,
but like an ivory hand reaching for dice
thrown across marble.
We roll and roll into the echo's
last chamber.

GLIMPSE INSIDE AN ARROW AFTER FLIGHT

Two arrows glanced off each other
flying in the same direction, both
still falling, though I have charge of the memory
that one struck the ground—as if memory
could retrieve it. But once on earth
we have the privilege of staying—for only then
are we able to outdistance
every living need
in something like a death. To seem
unpresent in our most ongoing
presence. How else could it happen
that I will never live long enough
to reach the other side
of this memory without you?

Name shouted down a well, name
of someone known and loved, name I say
in perfect faith I won't be answered—keep
your silence. If you spoke back
these things we have yet to mean
would have finished, would have
left us behind
as the past of a word in air.

LYNX LIGHT

The quilt has slipped
my shoulders. And when
you kiss the knots
in my fate like that
it's as if a lynx
co-exists with a housecat.

Give me winter for constancy
and looking back: most silent because
most decided.

Teach me how to shed
this cold devotion
by which memory
is exchanged for alertness.

Come and go with me—sickle,
black tail lashing this
                    transparent net of birdsong.

LIKE THE SIGH OF WOMEN'S HAIR

The horse stands under my window
but its rider is gone.
I know it's a vision. I know if
I went down to it and took it
by the mane, the breath it would blow
damp into my hair, breath sweet
as any man's who came to my door
with lovemaking on his mind,
would be muffled in dream.

How like the sigh of women's hair
as it falls to the floor in a glassy slicing,
his breath over me in the morning air.
All my windows were open,
the red winter grass high to his stirrup.
When he bent to me
I could hear the saddle creak, the horse
shifting under his thighs.

The grass, the wet grass across
my ankles when he pulled me
astride. "I'll tell you something
you won't forget in twenty years," he said,
like the last word before sleep.
"Tell me," I said.
But he didn't say more.
He wouldn't say more.
The horse took us down to the sea
and he wouldn't say more.

CAMEO

From her sly chariot drawn by cats
she has kept one as a moon
to her vermillioned eaves. She soars
in the checkered room, pulled along
by hair that rays out astonished
like the spiritual side of a tantrum,
or the mind's casual anatomy to either side
of a sudden, sprawling daydream.

Each hour is silver, is salt
to the enfolded extract of gaiety she gives off.
Why do we envy her ravaged nest between winter
and spring if not for its tender, vacant appeal—
as if to become more sweetly dark
we had stared with her into the cave
of a cello suspended by midday's unreality,
and had seen, in the silent curvature
of its spirit's kneeling,
the workings of a velvet moan.

BLACK VIOLETS

If I say "black violets" our first night
is nearly dark enough to draw this daylight rain
to memory's nomadic glistening, and I can
be there again, carrying love
to love in that room where his last heart
gave over its invisible amber. It's true,
he's evergreen in me and I make green use of him
to love you all the way back through death
into life again. I bury us in him and dig
us out again until we are a moon
that has passed through a mountain in order
to climb the night sky with no voice, no mouth,
no bodily empire except this lonely passage
for which he lends goodly silence and
the distance by which a moon can rise.

In that pang of earth you cast into me
he stepped forward, accompanied us
a little way into the present, into the sweetness
of so much yet to be lived out in this retrieval
of my unretrievable heart.
If you were two men to me there
it was to make lucid a fresh outlasting.
The one in which yours are the lips, yours
the enfolding vastness, this black rushing
of tiny fragrant faces against our skin, the violets
we feed each other petal by velvet
petal to keep the night long enough
for this new-made heart to open us in blood-darkness
into its farthest chamber.

ELEGY WITH A BLUE PONY

It is said one-third of China
is a cemetery: "But what
a cemetery!" Henri Michaux exclaimed.
Somewhere a cemetery exists
for all the kisses I was going to
give you. Multitudes of butterflies
like to sleep there in that third
of my heart's country. Their wings
open and shut pensively, as if
the lips of the sky had come down
to announce the end of a journey,
to ruffle the meadow grass
with the azure breeze of the moment.

If, in your travels in the spirit world,
you suddenly recall those kisses you
might have had, you won't have to
live again to enjoy them.
They are waiting. You will always
be expected by my kisses.
Lie down. Let the nose
of my blue pony brush your neck.
Don't be sad I'm not with her, or
that the butterflies rise as a body
to let her pass. Don't be sad.
I'm still alive and have to follow
my kisses around. But you, you can
lie down and be enlivened, kissed
into yet another imperishable
collaboration on the way to me.

from

My Black Horse

1995

> *I just want to ride my black horse,*
> *to see where he goes.*

T. G.
"LEGEND WITH SEA BREEZE"

To Whom Can I Open My Heart?

I step outside to get a clear view
of this night's first stars, but something
urgent and full of an ancient, inexplicable pain
is aloft in the darkness of the hemlocks.
Again and again it makes its shrill cry of panic
that is a plea and a question.
One bird after dark. What has befallen
its nest, its wing, its sun?
So little to tell. Not even the word *tomorrow*
is world enough to offer myself
hearing it.

URGENT STORY

When the oracle said, "If you keep pigeons
you will never lose home," I kept pigeons.
They flicked their red eyes over me,
a deft trampling
of that humanly proud distance
by which remaining aloof
is its own fullness. I administered
crumbs, broke sky with them like breaking

the lemon-light of the soul's amnesia
for what it wants but will neither take
nor truly let go. How it revived me,
to release them! And at that moment of flight
to disavow the imprint, to tear
their compasses out by the roots of
some green meadow they might fly over
on the way to an immaculate freedom, meadow

in which a woman has taken off
her blouse, then taken off the man's flannel shirt
so their sky-drenched arc
of one, then the other above
each other's eyelids is a branding of daylight,
the interior of its black ambush
in which two joys lame the earth a while
with heat and cloudwork under wing-beats.

Then she was quiet with him. And he
with her. The world hummed
with crickets, with bees nudging the lupines.
It is like that when the earth counts

its riches—noisy with desire
even when desire has strengthened our bodies
and moved us into the soak of harmony.

Her nipples in sunlight have crossed his palm
wind-sweet with savor and the rest
is so knelt before
that when they stand upright
the flight-cloud of my tamed birds shapes an arm
too short for praise. Oracle, my dovecot
is an over and over nearer to myself
when its black eyes are empty.
But by nightfall I am dark
before dark if one bird is missing.

Dove that I lost from not caring enough,
Dove left open by love in a meadow,
Dove commanding me not to know
where it sank into the almost-night—for you
I will learn to play the concertina,
to write poems full of hateful jasmine and
longing, to keep the dead alive, to sicken
at the least separation.
Dove, for whose sake
I will never reach home.

Because the Dream Is My Tenderest Arm

absence is a margin of strongholds. I go out
and I go out. Love is sequence and
condition: one of the few winter nights
it doesn't rain, one of the few
snowy mountains that refuses to
avalanche, one of my eternally suspended steps
that leads me, feeds me to the clean patch
of night outside his window
miles from where I lie sleeping.

Heart, he lies there sleeping. Heart, you are
only the shell of a confessed desire
wondering what to do next. The rules for love
in dreams command that all short-lived embryos
shaped by separations be dropped suddenly
onto his chest. Poem, you can die now.
He knows in the caverns of his dream's involuntary
memory that I tried to pass the faint expression
of these disheveled words over his body's echo.

Poem, put your breath down like a pen that knows
it is well used when the message is love,
when the poem has decayed into its heartbeat
and can be expressed simply as these petals I toss
through the dream's window
all night onto his sleeping face.

Heart, it doesn't matter. We were only sleeping
to let the poem know where to find us.
Now let it rain. Let the avalanche
of hours we've spent apart have their say. Only they

have the power to make these words
bear my heartprint as they fall outside the dream.

Poem, you can die now. I'm going to wake him
with my last petal. Now let it rain.
I want to leave a woman-sized body
outside his window with a dream's ambition:
never, no never to be filled
as this soul was with its body.

But if I speak of the soul,
it is only to use a halo of doubt
to mark the site of a true disappearance.

With Her Words beside Me

That cry of my friend who doesn't want
another woman to reap all she's sown
in a man. As if by guarding
we could keep love fast or at least safe
until it would grow true. But maybe love
is only a cat that goes where it's warm and
more casually tended, allowed
its come and go. I don't know.

I've lived both sides of guarding
and letting go, watched the lover rush backwards
or forwards to another, or accepted,
then treasured that one sent away
who was my joy and sweet reprieve.

Each time what I gave and took was mine
and not mine, as I am the lost work of footprints
scuffed into utterings overlapped
beyond claim in the dirt before the pay-shack.
Still I bend over her letter as over an abyss
out of which women's voices down the ages
lift to blister the night with ferocious resolve
to love until they are loved, themselves
the unadmitted bounty they could not keep.

From the solitary country of men
perhaps such ardent emissaries were also sent.
Imagine the road was long, the way
treacherous. Imagine, as we do,
that even now some are about to arrive.
Yes, I think so. A reciprocal wind

is blowing. I can smell carnations
out of my childhood, a sweet tearing
at the dialogue of the mysterious and the known.

Always these two insistent voices
and the wounded exceeding of women. Such men
they must be sending us!
Yes, I think so.

When the Enemy Is Illiterate

You must speak as St. Francis more than spoke
to the birds—with your hands out, upturned
to show you mean no harm. And, borrowing
a little wisdom from the trees, receive
everything that comes—strange nestings,
exorbitant winds, blind syllables of lightning,
tormented lovers carving their names
in the rough tablet of your lap.

Thus you will be obedient not to speech alone,
which is only the crude horizon upon which a mighty castle
was put to the torch and consumed
in a paralysis of over-exuberant, yet too solemn light.
Uncontending, you must yield intention so fully
that the template behind speech will sound
like a resplendent gong
above the aggrieved yet expectant face—its
closed radiance as the New Year confetti piles up
on your shoulders.

Finally, make yourself the site of a purposeful failure
to decipher harm in the frenzied economy
of any message. Remember virtue's unspoken strategy—
that we are put on earth as seriously as dreams,
as night and silence. The first star of the year
is always over our shoulders.
Take the splendid never-again path
which allows each clamped beak to divine
its surround of feathers.
Oh glad and fearful signs of bravest welcome.

FOR YVONNE

Yvonne McDonagh-Gaffney

Swept to her shoulders and out of the house—
the boys' sweaters, Granny's cardigan—that way
she had as a girl of borrowing
until we forgot to own. Now we coax her back
like a favorite garment that bears her scent,
laughter unraveling, like water breeze
pensive as a bride. How can she be
so everywhere and gone? Just like her to
store up warmth for us, stretching memory
like a sleeve until we are reshaped
by her absence. Coming upon *her* boat
marooned there on shore at Lough Arrow
is such wistfulness toward life
we know enough to turn it over,
climb in, let her hold us across the water.

UTTERLY

My spirit was a bee in those days—
the world one gigantic buzz, drooling
sweetness. Sweet unto bursting.
Love ahead. Love under me.

But most of all, that contrary ecstasy
ricocheting inside—the barren racket
love finally makes on its way to silence.

Utterly—to be destroyed in the kingdom
of flowers. Utterly sodden, sundered
into a blank of peace.
Not to remember outside caress
or tender look.

It's like that against the facelessness
of the heart. No contours. Only
unlivable crimson. Only the clustered braille
of a fearless premonition
fumbling the turned cheek.

No, Not Paradise

When the mouth of the lion unhinges
in paradise, do his teeth gleam
with a frenzied trembling left over
from death, that unripe windowpane
we press our faces against to admire
the roofless serenity of beings at ease
with the perpetual?

Or the woman—whose back might as well
be a mountain in profile for how it wears
its stars without looking up—does she
never weep for love like a bonfire
in that undulating consummation of new days?
And if her thighs are immaculate,
will the moon borrow passion
from the heron's blue lament?
And what of her: Shall I go? Shall I stay?

Rather to feast on the raw heart of a dream
in which our animal souls pare away
an earthly sadness so omnipotent
we startle awake, ungentled
as lake water at midnight
whose stars, even in repose, know
they will never be confirmed.
No, not paradise, but the lion's rich red look.

LAUGHTER AND STARS

I didn't make present
those days he didn't complain
but I knew he was sick, felt
sick, and a look would pass between us,
a doomed look that nonetheless
carried streamers of light like a comet
scratching light across the tablet of the night sky.
We looked into each other
and like the comfort a small branch is to a bird
on a long migration, we took comfort in
the two-way knowing of that look.

I didn't make present enough
his beautiful will as he went to his room
with the fireplace and heaped the fire up
to match the inner burning of his body's candle,
the cells igniting so fast by then
it kept him awake, pacing him wall to wall
in the cage of his body's luster like a panther
of the will, supple and searching its parameters.
He fed the fire; he wrote
                              poems.

No, I couldn't make present
the tender way he took my body in the night
into his arms, holding his one radiance to me
like a wet match upon which one
dry spot remained and he turned just so and struck himself
against me and there was a blazing up, the way the night
ignites with more than lips and parted legs

when two souls
in their firefly selves
come together asking
to be buried in the no-song-left-but-this
                                    dark.

Had I been able to give these things
I might have described his innocent laughter
with a friend and me the night before his death, laughter
at the clumsiness of the body, his body,
with the oxygen tank attached, making sure the tube
was in his mouth. His wanting to go out onto
the deck of the house to see the stars again. The wheelchair
catching on the rug, the oxygen tank
trying to jolt loose, but somehow everything jangling along
out the sliding glass doors, and the sky huge
with a madman's moon, huge as a man's heart on its last
breath-beat so we had to shield ourselves
and turn away to find the
                                    stars.

Such a plaintive, farewell hissing
they made, like diamonds imbedded
in the blue-black breast of forever. But then
it was the night before my love's last morning,
and we were together, one body to another, laughter
and stars, laughter and stars.

Then he got up, stood up with everything still attached and we
helped him hack open a bright crevasse in the night, to hurl

his heart-beat like the red living fist it was
one more time
out across the sleeping thresholds
of the living.

Two Bracelets

I wear on my left arm—one
of silver, the other gold.

I am your silver.
You are my gold.
My gold in you.
In me, your silver.

When I slip on my dress
in the morning, when I take it off
in the dark, my gold
clicks against your silver.
I hear it in my farthest
cave. You hear it
wherever you are and pause
as if a wing-shadow
had passed over your heart.

Why is it me? Why is it you?
My gold, my silver—how
can I know? At my wrist
the beaten silver
riding the hammered gold.
It is you. It is me.

I arrange my hair, lift it high
off my neck. My gold
slips over my silver. What
does it know of reasons.
Love is strong enough not to know.

I chop the wood for our fire.
Inside the blow of the axe-edge
the wood breaks open. My arm
forgets its silver, its gold—though,
like a small silver cry
something has carried its gold
into the stricken air, something
is speaking, a sparkling that echoes.

Inscription of light issuing from what
I have given myself in your name,
in your most unspoken
name, the one the world
will pierce with arrows, the one
without answers, the name
I don't know how to call you
except like a woman
so unbound to her love
she puts her body through the hoop of it
every time she reaches or
turns, and the love
is daily and splendid
that she chooses inside his
choosing, that asks him to give over,
that he gives over, and brings out
of their joining—now
silver, now gold.

Why is it me? Why is it you?
My bracelets in their chattering.
Each time they touch

is the right time.
This love, it's an ambush of unison.
My most unspoken, my cloudy silver—gold
unfathomable.

CHILD SINGING

Where were we going? Destination fades
in music. The one thing left of that night
in a darkened car—her singing, how it came
from her like breath made audible, yet happened
to her and not for anyone. If the car
had been rolling along with only herself
in the back seat, she would have been singing.

That time dissolved now, swirled
into pure voice, as memory itself effortlessly
allows us to reach altitude, the way
walking alone in mountains
makes songs easy to recall. Those times
the heart lodged inside memory
breaks through the barriers of raw decision
that plague it with fault. In song
the invented continuity falls away
like a hand used alternately to shield,
then bare the eyes in mountain sun.

But her face in darkness,
her braided, golden hair in darkness, wore
our listening so it turned to singing, as it had to.
Rough cargo of forgetfulness, buoyant
as the head of a poppy, we rushed along
with her as down a streambed distant, a mind
having to gentle itself
against its own shadows.
These word-ghosts of witnessing,

to know simply that some things are ideal
and must be left so.

There was singing.
We never reached home.

for Rijl

Iris Garden in May

Seen from the road, a herd of sea horses
spoils towards night under the cherry trees.
Like the mind of their gardener, they swim
sun-shadowed continents in place. Each bloom's
aperture rules an unruly cathedral, love
clowning the sword hilt. Chalice-like
the standard cups after-rain, casques of impulse
eager to shake us wet with vigilante droplets

as we follow her cautiously. Unlike Saint Teresa
she won't be bribed toward affection
with a sardine. She beheads her Decoration Day
bouquet, prefers hybrids which stretch the rainbow
past color to the under-language of hues and scents.
Heaped with moonlight or plucked suddenly
from the icy spine of winter, they stab into earth
like ardor. If the Rainbow Goddess sent this cavalry

to heaven, the message would be flag-handsome
with new-moon audacity. Ask the gardener if she
has anything to do with their Renaissance velvet,
she answers an imbecile: "Why sure!"
She admires their not being gradual, sidereal,
digressive as she—for to open all at once
surpasses mere beauty by infinities of welcome.
Where we step, the bulb, chicken-footed, shows

through soil as if to taunt joy with sinister
origins. So long a widow, her litany recognizes
black as congratulatory: *Hello Darkness,* its obsidian

purple-black, *Houdini's* cherry undertones, dark burgundy
of *Black Tornado,* or the falls of *Tabriz* tantalizing

like moth's wings. And there—her tallest black, coveted
by the visitor, never to be cut: *Black Out.*

for Georgia Morris (Quigley) Bond

Dear Ghosts,

2006

> . . . *black butterflies of the general soul,*
> *join me to those who are missing, those who sleep*
> *like hives of wild honey, who sleep with their*
> *sweetness intact like a blue door, sure and firm,*
> *in the swift corridors of the night.*

T. G.
"DEAR GHOSTS,"

My Unopened Life

lay to the right of my plate
like a spoon squiring a knife, waiting
patiently for soup or the short destiny
of dessert at the eternal picnic—unsheltered
picnic near the mouth of the sea
that dares everything forgotten to huddle
at the periphery of a checked cloth spread
under the shadowy, gnarled penumbra
of the madrona.

Hadn't I done well enough with the life
I'd seized, sure as a cat with
its mouthful of bird, bird with its
belly full of worm, worm like an acrobat of darkness
keeping its moist nose to the earth, soaring
perpetually into darkness without so much as
the obvious question: why all this darkness?
And even in the belly of the bird: *why
only darkness?*

The bowl of the spoon
collects entire rooms just lying there next
to the knife. It makes brief forays into
the mouth delivering cargoes of ceilings
and convex portraits of teeth
posing as stalactites of
a serially extinguished cave

from whence we do nothing but stare out
at the sea, collecting little cave-ins of
perception sketched on the moment

to make more tender the house of the suicide
in which everything was so exactly
where it had been left by someone missing.
Nothing, not even the spoon he abandoned
near the tea cup, could be moved without
seemingly altering the delicious
universe of his intention.

So are we each lit briefly by engulfments
of space like the worm in the beak of
the bird, yielding to sudden corridors
of light-into-light, never asking: *why,*
tell me why
        all this light?

NOT A SPARROW

Just when I think the Buddhists
are wrong and life is not mostly suffering,
I find a dead finch near the feeder.
How sullen, how free of regret, this death
that sinks worlds. I bury her near
the bicycle shed and return to care for
my aged mother, whose suffering
is such oxygen we do not consider it,
meaning life at any point exceeds
the price. A little more. A little more.

That same afternoon, having restored balance,
I discover a junco fallen on its back, beak
to air, rain pelting the prospect. Does
my feeder tempt flight through windows?
And, despite evidence, do some
accomplish it?

Digging a hole for the second bird, I find
the first gone. If I don't think "raccoons"
or "dogs," I can have a quiet, unwitnessed
miracle. Not a feather remains.
In goes the junco. I swipe earth over it,
set a pot on top. Time
to admit the limitations of death as
admonition.

Still, two dead birds in an afternoon
lets strange sky into the mind: birds flying
through windows, flying through
earth. Suffering must be like that too: equipped

with inexplicable escapes where the mind
watches the hand level dirt over the emptied grave
and, overpowered by the idea of wings,
keeps right on flying.

SAH SIN

I found the hummingbird
clutched in torpor
to the feeder on the day
my student from long ago
appeared. I sent him into
the house and tried to
warm it, lifting my blouse
and caching it—(as I'd heard
South American women do)
under a breast.

It didn't stir, but I held it there
like a dead star for a while
inside my heart-socket
to make sure, remembering the story
of a mother in Guatemala
whose baby had died
far from home. She pretended
it was living, holding it
to her breast the long way
back on the bus, so no one
would take it from her before
she had to give it over.
When the others on the journey
looked across the aisle
they saw only a mother and
her sleeping child, so tenderly
did she hold the swaddled form.

Miles and miles we flew
until I knew what that breast

was for when the form
of your not-there arrived. We
were impenetrably together
then, as that mother and child
must have been, reaching home at last,
her child having been kept alive
an extra while by the tender glances
of strangers.

Inside, my student and I found
a small cedar box
with a Nootka salmon
painted onto its glass lid.
I told him of the dead
hummingbirds people saved
in their freezers because
they found them too beautiful
to bury. We made a small mausoleum
for *Sah Sin* under the sign
of the salmon, so the spear of her beak
could soar over death a while longer.
Next we propped the box
on the window ledge
facing out toward the mountains.

Then we went on about
our visit. My student
had become famous in the East
for his poems. Now he was
a little bored with being
a poet. He asked some questions

about what I might be
writing—courteously, as one
inquires about someone
not considered for a while.
I made a pot of tea
and served it in the maroon cups
the size of ducks' eggs
so it would take
a long while to drink. Fame.
It was so good to sit
with him. He seemed
to have miraculously survived
every hazard to make his way
to my house again.

Choices

I go to the mountain side
of the house to cut saplings,
and clear a view to snow
on the mountain. But when I look up,
saw in hand, I see a nest clutched in
the uppermost branches.
I don't cut that one.
I don't cut the others either.
Suddenly, in every tree,
an unseen nest
where a mountain
would be.

for Drago Štambuk

FIRE STARTER

For a year I am an only child running into
the winter glare. My father, a pipe-fitter
in the Bremerton shipyard, leaves the bed in darkness
to work a second job. In my mother's remembering
he slips from warmth not to wake us.
Soon, like a thief who belongs, he enters,
one after the other, the neighborhood houses, before
the families are up. He gathers
what he needs to lay the fire
in each stove, then strikes a match
to set it going, so when they rise
from sleep, the house will have the chill off
and a fire crackling. Such work is his
because these southern transplants
don't yet know what will catch fire
in the damp of hemlock, fir and alder.

My young father, newly arrived himself
from coal mines and cotton fields
to the Northwest, carrying fire, hearth to hearth,
in a time when no one locks their doors.
House to house he clears ashes, crumpling
news of war: *June 6, 1944.*
ALLIES INVADE EUROPE.
In a calculated toss, he
adds kindling split the night before, builds
the loose crisscross cedar scaffolding
for fire to climb, mindful that even flames
must breathe—leaving space for breaths,
in his absence, to be drawn.

He does this before I know what fire is, how it
arcs back to caves and clearings,
our ancestral huddlings.

I am nearly a year old.
The first nuclear bomb is being readied to drop
on Hiroshima and, *for good measure,* Nagasaki.
It is something of which my father
will never speak—so far beyond his ken,
the use of people, their homes, as incidental
combustibles. What news of Nazi ovens
he had, or what he thought, I do not
know. Only that Europe
was always over there,
and he didn't need to see it, asking me later
Are you sure you have to go over there?

My father on his knees
in the sleeping house, trying not
to wake the babies, and beneath
the dull clang of wood against metal
the muffled sounds of lovemaking, or
the low murmur of the night's dream-cargo
exchanged between husband and wife, or
the husband gone to work, the mother
a room away, child at her breast, swaddled
in the after-warmth of their night's accumulated
heat. Trust then, sure as the flare
of the wooden match.

My young fire-starter father
has done his work. The street he leaves
uncoils white plumes scribbling
the damp air, signs of life rising
from the chimneys of the wood-framed houses,
as if each had a comic-book voice for a comic-book
time in which war was going to succeed,
after which an eagle would sift down
into the hemlock, the men would come home
under confetti, and women, laying aside
their welding tools, would again disguise themselves
with aprons. A time in which horrors might
be stopped by the quick fix of war.

My flesh-and-blood father
glances back at the peace of his neighborhood
to which he has added one small, necessary magic: fire.
The lights are going on. Households are stirring.
The sweet wood-smoke nostalgia of democracy
hangs over the town.

for Leslie Bond (1907–1982)

Little Match Box

And if there were two moons,
who would sleep when one
passed before the other
and took it in
on its dark side? Wouldn't
some extra light ray out
around the sustaining one?
Wouldn't you sense
the two in one, even if you'd
never seen them parted?

Sometimes a glory
is just that—a guessing-into
the seen, noticing
the fringe of presence
when it comes, trying to match
its fervency by something
as tangible, something
only you are equal to.

THE WOMEN OF AUSCHWITZ

were not treated so well as I.
I am haunted by their shorn heads,
their bodies more naked for this
as they stumble against each other
in those last black-and-white
moments of live footage.

Before she cuts the braid
Teresa twines the red ribbon
bordered with gold into my hair.
The scissors stutter against the thick
black hank of it, though for its part,
the hair is mute.

When it was done
to them they stood next to each other.
Maybe they leaned
into each other's necks afterwards. Or
simply gazed back with the incredulity
of their night-blooming souls.

Something silences us.
Even the scissors, yawing at
the anchor rope, can't find their sound.
They slip against years as if they were bone.
I recall an arm-thick rope I saw in China
made entirely of women's hair, used to anchor
a ship during some ancient war
when hemp was scarce.

At last the blades come together
like the beak of a metallic stork,

delivering me into my new form.
The braid-end fresh and bloodless.
Preempting the inevitable,
Teresa uses the clippers to buzz off
the rest. Breath by plover-breath, hair
falls to my shoulders, onto the floor, onto
my feet, left bare for this occasion.

As the skull comes forward,
as the ghost ship
of the cranium, floating
in its newborn ferocity, forces through,
we are in no doubt: the helm
of death and the helm of life
are the same, each craving light.

She sweeps the clippings onto the dust pan
and casts them from the deck
into the forest. Then, as if startled awake,
scrambles down the bank
to retrieve them, for something live
attaches to her sense of hair, after
a lifetime cutting it.

I am holding nothing back.
Besides hair, I will lose toenails, fingernails,
eyelashes and a breast to the ministrations
of medicine. *First you must make
the form,* Setouchi-san tells me, explaining
why the heads of Buddhist nuns are shaved.
The shape is choosing me, simplifying,

shaving me down to essentials,
and I go with it. Those women
of Auschwitz who couldn't choose—
Meanwhile the war plays out
in desert cities, the news shorn of images
of death and dismemberment.

I make visible the bare altar
of the skull.
Time is deepened. Space
more intimate than
I guessed. I run my hand over
the birth-moment I attend sixty years
after. I didn't know the women
would be so tender. Teresa takes my
photograph in Buddha Alcove, as if to prove
the passage has been safe. Holly, Jill, Dorothy,
Alice, Suzie, Chana, Debra, Molly and Hiromi offer flowers
and a hummingbird pendant, letting me know
they are with me. My sister
is there and Rijl.

I feel strangely gentled, glimpsing
myself in the mirror, the artifact
of a country's lost humility.
My moon-smile, strange and far,
refuses to belong to the cruelties
of ongoing war. I am like a madwoman
who has been caught eating pearls—softly radiant,
about to illuminate a vast savanna, ready
to work a miracle with everything left to her.

SURGEON

He's sketching the shape
of the incision across my left
breast. *What about my heart?*
I can't help asking.
*Oh, don't worry. We'll leave
that.* He smiles.
A *bat wing* he calls the design
he'll use to lift the breast from
the chest wall. *Thanks, doc,
for giving me half my boyhood
back,* I tell him from the gurney,
thinking to relieve his scalpel
of hesitation. Then I'm under.

Afterwards, high on pain meds,
I talk on the phone
to loved ones in an exuberant
soaring and don't recall a thing.
Strange to put my hand
there days later and find only
the pouting lip.

Suzie tending the wound
after my night's respite
in hospital. She's left her easel
to minister. Alfredo up and
down from the basement where
he's been painting dream-jungles,
checking on me, asking sweetly
in his own healing mantra:
Tessita-how-you do-*ing?*

My third operation in a year and
Suzie's confident now, knows
how to manage this. Like a bewildered
child, I surrender to comfort
when she tucks me in at night.
Don't talk to me of heaven.

for Susan Lytle and Alfredo Arreguín

THE RED DEVIL

the nurses on the cancer ward call it
because, like acid, if it spills
from the needle onto skin, the patient
has to have a skin graft. Red devil
for how it singes the inside of
the veins, causes the hair to fall
out and the nails of the hands and feet
to lift from their beds, to shrivel
or bunch like defective armor.

Now the test reveals the heart
pumps 13% less efficiently.
Never mind. Your heart
was a superheart anyway.
Now it's normal. Join
the club. Get tired. Learn to nap.
Watch the joggers loping uphill
as if under water, as if
they had something to teach you
about the past, how sweet
and useless it was, taking the stairs
two at a time. They still
call you *hummingbird*.
Sooner or later you'll be flying
on your back to prove
you've got at least
one trick left.

BULL'S-EYE

Driving to the ferry,
that reverie releasing
the unsaid, I tell my friend
it's okay. I'll be okay.
When the doctor
said *There's no cure*
an arrow flew out of
the cosmos—*thung!*
Heart's center. Belonging
to everything. That
quick.

for Valerie

ORANGE SUTRA

I wanted to take you in, peel and all,
with the mind's all-swallowing.
But the mind prefers unoranging
the orange until a segment unhinges
to shine upright
in the night sky, unaware
of the night or of its own shining.

So the mind makes a darker thing
of night's conception of itself.
To be *at crescent* admonishes lamentation
as a temporary setback. Mindful
of the round, of the moon's fullness—the night,
encroaching, also draws power
to increase or disappear
into us, entirely.

Gone full again, how orange are you, Orange,
now that a moon mistakes you
for its daughter? Just as I thought: you are
a wisecrack in the abundance of night's spiraling
obituary, willing to carry us
with you like poor relations until
we run out of pretexts and gambits.

If I choose to live in mind of you,
I can know you only by a sideways glimpse,
the blackboard-staccato of a thought's mad
all-over grammar, those woolly bees
of the heart that want to sting a moment to death
with memory—spelling the past *wuz,*

with its fur on, and letting it roll before us
like an orange, a portable altar
that prays all over itself
with itself.

You could say so, Orange.
You could kneel as you said so.
The way an orange is always kneeling
and upright at once.

DREAM DOUGHNUTS

Mother, I'm so glad
      to see you again! for she had been dead some while.
Oh my son! she says, kissing him, *I'm also glad*
      to see you!
I have so much to tell you, he says.
      Tell me, then.
Not now, mother, he says. *We have so much time.*

At the Parisian restaurant Pierre tells his dream
of meeting his dead mother. Sebastian, the jazz musician,
says he's giving up drink, going to take better care
of himself. It's time he *found a nice girl and settled down,*
had some children. Two young mathematicians at the table
discuss logic which I'm always hijacking
with metaphor and image. I tell them how I read Ray's
book of poems cover to cover until he entered
my dream as through some side-door in the jazz club,
some loophole in time.

I'm so glad to see you again, I say.
He's carrying a bag of powdered doughnuts
and two paper cups of black coffee.
Was I gone too long? he asks, fresh from the bakery.
Too long is if you don't come back at all, I say.
Time is funny, he says, biting into the doughnut
so the hole breaks open to the entire air supply
of the planet. Powdered sugar clings to the corners
of his lips. *Ghost-lips* I call him, as he
tears off doughnut and feeds it to me like a small bird
who won't eat any other way. Time,

like the doughnut hole, has rejoined itself,
as when joining breaks us open to ourselves, corollary
to *again.*

I say to Ray:
> *Did you ever think*
> *it would be like this?*
> *Drink your coffee,* he says, *while it's hot.*

For a while we're all out there together, but soon
I know I'll have to go back to that alcove
in which we're always waiting to see
each other again, the one we call Life, so it has
a hole in the middle, a sign of arrival, given
so we don't need to miss ourselves or anyone else,
we're that sure the whole,
in some unaccountable lightning-flash-hyphenation,
goes on and on, as it takes
our very breath away.

for Maya

You Are Like That,

a moon, and then the night sky
around the moon, a violet-blue
made whole by phases
as the moon tries to submerge itself and
fails. Why do you pretend to go,
then surge back a slice at a time, just when
I've given you up? Sometimes fog washes in
from the strait and you are entirely
gone. What is it like to be
so *gone?* Do you feel my moth-mind fumbling
you up there in the dark?
I'm like the schoolgirl at the back of the class
who can't help raising her hand toward the ceiling
even when she can't answer
the question, lifting herself
by desire alone.

Do you care about questions? Or are you
both sides of the moon-coin now, subduing
even chance? One night in a car I raced
beside you up the mountains,
just to rise with you for once, instead of
like now, drifting toward my own night,
wondering if I can stay missing long enough
to discover sleep's lost, alternate door, the one
round as a moon with no threshold—
a door so open it's hard to find, even
when you do. Did passing through
happen something like that,
just because a dying occurred? or was dying itself
greedily restorative on its far side? or

was it better than any detective story: a charmed opening,
casual as a teacher pointing
to the lucky one who gets to erase
the blackboard, except for a few yellow half-
words at the top which can only partly
be reached and so are freed to
float there for days like the left-over ghost
of a conjugation: *He was. I am.*

Open, like half of any-
thing: the way a tree,
even in a treachery of moon-
light, never worries about having enough
birds. Or, in the fullness of day-
light, that unspecific opening
that lets us import-
antly half-see
when the question, as it reaches,
knows it isn't
tall enough.

Oil Spot

A blue-black planet, it falls from
the chainsaw into rainwater
puddled where the earthquake
left its shoulders in the driveway,
the depression in gravel
reminding us we walk on waves.

The droplet flings itself down, radiates
like a jellyfish unfurling its
mantle—filtrating, rippling.
At its core, a violet eye,
magenta-lashed, its milky skirting
buoyant.

Josie goes into the house
for the camera to take its portrait.
The door to beauty always
stands open. Days later he stares
at the photograph until it enters
him fully, just a spot of oil,
transforming his hand
with its paint brush
into an instrument of rainbow
approximations that begin to pale
the original.

Like a satellite moon
the eyelet center deeply shines.
Planet-Josie revolves over
it, the light of his face
also entering as he works.

Beauty passes through us
blackly shuddering, stabilizes
its revolution and, against
all expectation, begins to rise from
the undulating shape
on his page.

A heart like that
at eighty.

for Josie Gray, b. March 23, 1925

Moon's Rainbow Body

Forbidden to travel by night,
you nonetheless arrive
at dawn. In Josie's portrait
I attend your birth moment,
accomplished in a swirl
of greens against a night sky
of green. Where did he
get you, green moon, and
by what permission do you
make a birth out of
a seeming disintegration?

Like a thumb print
on glass, you hover
in daylight, marking the sky
with a scar of midnight.
Suddenly my body leaps
with you into the immensity,
so gone the word *gone*
can't find a mouth
to say it. Each moonlit

arrival is like a gong
without a temple
reverberating against
an unseen mountain.
The spider's mouth
unravels a silken bridge
across which the fly
belies it ever
flew.

DEAR GHOSTS,

my friend is back from Cairo.
He is tired in the eyes from all he has seen.
Tired too from drinking whiskey straight
in the little dusty cafés, keeping up with the company.
It is 1991, before the bad business
of Iraq, of Afghanistan, before my own time in Cairo.

We drink a little whiskey together,
joining one far midnight to another, because
my black-haired orphan is with us—she whose brown eyes
add a crackling to the night. Her glances,
black butterflies of the general soul, join me to one
who is missing, who sleeps like a hive of wild honey
with his sweetness intact like a blue door,
sure and firm, in the swift corridors
of the night. He who tries to wrest shards of love
from the world in broad daylight, who loves
only a little at first, then madly.

Love, such a run-down subject, says the ancient poet
of Rio. My orphan smiles and clicks
her whiskey glass to mine.

In Cairo the camels throw the weight of their haunches
onto their knees and rise up. An old man passes through
the café swinging from a chain his brass cylinder
embossed with stars and half moons.
The charred droplets of burnt musk rain over us,
seep through our sleeves onto our skin.
My friend is talking about his Italian motorcycle.

Love, such a run-down subject, especially,
forced as I am, to mix these living creatures
with ghosts, with the axe-edge beauty
of a woman's indifference and the sleeping lips
of that one who lies even more deeply asleep in me.

Suddenly the bar is noisy, the music
a raw throb at the base of the brain. We can't talk
about love or anything else in here. Time
to put our arms around each other's waists—my man,
my woman, my unapproachable dream.
Time to walk out into the pungent streets of Cairo
with kisses of good night on a street corner
where it is dark and cool enough
for weddings that happen all night long
to the frantic pulse of the *tabla.* Move back, the men
are dancing, the men are showing their sex
in their hips, their bellies and waists. Rose water
is splashing our brows on this street corner, unappointed
as we are, but bound inexactly by whiskey,
loud music, Italian motorcycles, by the unknown
parents of my orphan.

And in the wide silence of each step,
the implosive blue rose drops unknowingly
into my thigh to preserve love's ache, love's
incandescent whisper under the black smell of mountains.
And I don't know why
we are together, dear ghosts, or why
we have to part. Only that it is precious
and that I love
this run-down subject.

KNIVES IN THE BORROWED HOUSE

Don't sharpen them.
Expectation, more dangerous
than any blade.

SUGARCANE

Some nights go on in an afterwards so secure
they don't need us, though sometimes one exactly
corresponds to its own powers of elemental tirelessness.
A prodigious heaviness comes over it that upswings it
into taking us, like the seizure knowing is,
back into its mouth. One blue-violet night in Hawaii during
the Vietnam War pinions me against

the war's prolonged foreboding as I relive it yet
in the preposterous homecoming the generals arranged
for their men on R & R in that meant-to-be paradise. Wives
flown in to bungalows and beach-side hotels, their suitcases
crammed with department-store negligees for conjugal trysts
that seem pornographic now in their psycho-erotic
rejuvenation of the killing. But he

was my husband. And I was glad he hadn't gone down
in a craze of flak in some widow-maker out of Da Nang
zigzagging over to Cambodia to drop its load. Glad
my government had a positive view of sexual continuity,
wanted its men in loving arms at their war's halftime.
We would meet, as some would not. Seven months gone—
daily letters, tapes and that telepathic hotline reserved
for saints and gods, except when women's wartime
solicitations to their mates usurp all tidy elevations.
But what did

those heavenly bodies, those angel currents, make of so much
heavy panting and suppositional boudoir?
Or of homeward-yanking fantasies interspersed
with napalm, sniper fire, firebombing, mines—the dead,

the wounded lifted out by helicopter?
I would see you in and out of khaki
again. Was early to the island, tanning a luxurious khaki
into my sallow in a luminescent bikini after months
working the dawn shift on a medical ward.
But the night is tired of its history
and doesn't know how we got here. Children

are what it wants. Though we didn't know it, no amount of
innocent gladness of the young to meet again on earth
would bring them back. Nor could they be revived
in the glower of long rain-shattered afternoons as we labored
to push ourselves back into each other.
They were gone from us, those children.
As if disenfranchisements like this were some mercurial,
unvoiceable by-product of the country's mania, its payment
in kind for those flaming children

we took into the elsewhere. There was so much to spare you
I had to overuse loving as balm, a cauterizing
forgetfulness to prise you to me. Maybe the exuberance
of our stretching all the way to first-love, that *always*
to each other, allowed our lack its comfortless posture,
and we were given respite in which a quiet light
thought us human enough to slough off its breath-saddened
anguish. And then I saw you

made new again in moonlight. Not as yourself, but as
more entirely made of pain in its power
of always usurping what might also
be true. As I was true in moonlight, preparing to meet you,

lifted by the raw gaiety of my brother's shipmates
taking shore leave the night before you touched down,
the gleeful carload of us emptied into a field
because I'd never tasted sugarcane.
Breaking off the chalky stalks,

my juiceless sucking and licking the woody fiber
in darkness, the flat way it discarded me, as if another, greedier
mouth had been there first. Then the young man's voice,
my hand with his around it lifted, so he tore with his biting
the stalk I held, squeezing my hand until the full pressure
of his jaw passed into me
as what was needed for sweetness to yield.

And since sweet pressure is all I gave—that boy's
unguarded kiss in moonlight was yours, was any god's invitation
to how we'd meant our love to close us,
close, in a little rest, allowing
that sweet scythe of unfoulable kindred tenderness, before
the rest. That biting down on us.
The heavy pressure that demands its sweetness as it mouths
and sucks, until it finds us with its love-letting teeth.

WEATHER REPORT

The Romanian poets
under Ceausescu, Liliana
said, would codify opposition

to the despots in this manner: because
there was no gas and they were cold, everyone
was cold, all they had to do was write

how cold it is . . . so cold . . . and their
readers knew exactly what was meant.
No one had to go to jail
for that.

Liliana, in the dead of night
writing her poems
with gloves on.

I think I'll take off my gloves.
It's freezing in here.
There's a glacier pressing on my heart.

America 2001–2009

ETERNAL

"So what," he says. He's
fifteen, has seen heads
blown from bodies—legs,
arms, entrails strewn.
"So what." He is clutching
a rifle, leveling his
no-man's-land black eyes
into the camera.

He's been fighting for years.
Something mirthful
plays at the corners
of his mouth. If the camera
turned into a gun
he would empty his rifle
into the cameraman
with his last breath.
And even as he breathes it
he won't believe
it's his last.

He hasn't belonged
to himself perhaps ever.
A last breath is what the living
worry about. He isn't a thing
like that. He's a soul
who craves bullets. Looking into him
is like staring into
a small clenched sun.

And so you finally see him,
dulled on his haunches
by your shadow. And you become
for a moment some vagabond god,
and you bless him. That's
what gods are for.

Okay. Now withdraw
the god. Withdraw
the blessing. That's how it's done.
The emptying out
of several words, two
souls, many gods.

Only human.
Bullet. Bullet. Bullet.
Dead. Only dead.
Are you with me?

EMANATION OF THE RED CHILD

Child that never existed
because to exist
is to need the world
as a place merely to enter
as a leaving. Child
the horse's legs stepped through
crossing the river; how you kept
the red of you in the river-flow
so as always to be seen, the not-sure
of you gathering, undulating
edgeless and the rider
swinging down from the stirrup
to stand waist high in you
as you dissipated and reformed
like a fish flexing its
river-muscle. Child pulling light
into a tattered guess-work shawl
under trees. Spirit-shout
whose echo refuses its assignment
of incremental leave-taking and so
gains stature, agreeing to stay
fringed with loss just glancing
off promise. We enter the inexplicable
where the child's delight exceeds
what can be seen by anyone looking on.

So the red child exceeds our thought
of it, envelopes eagerly the shimmering
notion of the horse's nostrils sifting its
water-garden of breath-lilies where
no birth can empty it and no death

ever drink its fill. Red child
finding a way to be and not be
like a riderless horse
letting the river fall from its flanks
as it gains the bank
and its horse-mind catches the glint
of light in water where a stirrup,
the steely brand of it marks
the red-child-moment
and is empty, so empty
we keep on seeing
what can't be
seen.

for Tiernan

SHE WIPES OUT TIME

like shaking horseflies from her white mane.
She would like to mail a postcard to
the place she was born. Not just to anyone,
but to the postmaster. *When I stopped to*
see him he'd gone out into his fields.
He had forty acres, she says. *I didn't*
go looking for him. I gaze across America, across
death to the postmaster, walking
his Missouri fields—wide sweep of farmland,
walnut groves, rivers and once-inhabited Indian caves
gouged into hillsides I explored
as a child by horseback.

A thousand acres, my mother says, restoring
them to herself and bequeathing them
to her children. *Your grandfather has a thousand acres.*
That sentence still a kingdom. The land gone,
but the words of it sustaining,
as if those acres—the vibratory memory
of them—were somehow currency to feeling able
for an expanse of loss. But who needs
a thousand acres? Better to have the thought
without the bother, to walk the mind under walnut trees
on the slope behind a barn long since
fallen away—as the mind falls away—the roots
exposed so the dry tendrils of small bushes
that cling bird-footed to air
remind us that air itself is a soil
apparitional to desire.

I too want to go back. Do go,
through the long stride of her wish
to make this sign of remembrance: a postcard
to the postmaster. In my mother's memory
of home, on which I lean, the postmaster still walks .
his forty acres, though I know he is
long dead. Is it cruel to tell her
and obliterate that switchback
her yearning makes to resurrect him—who now
represents a place she can't quite reach
in her mind, except through the hyphenated corridor
of his perpetual looming up
as one broken promise?
I said I'd stop and see him . . . calm disappointment
in her voice. Any god would let this postmaster
have his saunter in the mind-works of another. I say
nothing, let him live, beckoning to us both
across time, death and any upstart moment
that chooses her.

I am attracted to this new fold in time
by which a postmaster escapes death through having
gone for a walk. But I want her with me.
"Mother," I ask, "when did you last see him?"
Her voice has the lilt of truth. Memory's strange accordion
crumples expertly under the tail of the monkey:
Oh, a couple years ago.
"Mother, it's twenty years since you were back."
Then, making her arrow sing: *How time flies!*

By custodial violence I yank her to my template,
offer the card she wanted to send.
She forgets what it was for, uses it all day
as a page marker in her handbook
on African violets. Later she
reads deliciously aloud: *Water them*
from the top and you'll rot the crown. Always
let them take what they need
from the bottom.

Language itself has flown
defensively from the page into her
mouth with the audacity of particulate, unquenchable
matter that is, at any moment, fully able
to restore girlish laughter
to the high veranda, the postmaster's hand
closing vast distances
to my father's courtship letters,
ten years handing them over to her—letters
from her lover, far away in the desperate burrowings
of the coal mines. And now depths darker.
Twenty years toiling under us in the black ore of absence,
as the violets drink on their sills
from little bowls of the mind.

for Georgia Morris (Quigley) Bond

The Violence of Unseen Forms

". . . oh how I long just once to feel
the hand within me that throws larks
so high into the sky"

LETTER FROM RILKE

Can one soul consume
another? Or does asking violate
the notion: soul inviolable?
To ask is to wonder anew at the violence
of unseen forms.

Was it will over will?
Or did superior need bend us, one to
another? Does one who serves
hold the upper hand, having failed purposefully,
in the small ways, to mark and seal
parameters?

Is there loss?
Or does the soul-inside-the-soul
resort to bird song, to the shadow-languages
of touch and glance at its central core,
preferring undertow as it
more graciously attends
the world's day by day.

When one soul takes on the heft
of a faltering soul
is it transaction, translation, atonement
or all three—for which the deeds themselves
are gratefully forfeit
to the renewed essence of both?

All I know is, when her soul
seemed to fail her, I had no choice.
In the lifting up I became another
venturing, could shake far cries in realms
unguessed. Nor could I return
without the shade of her
who carried me into her need, beyond
mere mercies.

Only then did the deeper hand in me
learn to throw larks
for sheer pleasure: to feel them climb sky
to heights never touched otherwise,
and for no reason. Just, inexplicably, we could.
And with that release
the violence, against all prediction,
ended.

ACROSS THE BORDER

Into early morning we circle
the problem of his mother's dementia,
her cries of *help me! help me!*
ricocheting against stars
even from the balcony of this posh hotel
across the Canadian border
where he and his family are like refugees
of some secret war-torn country
within the country. I sit with him
the way a mountain sits with another
mountain, comparing weather,
the slippage of glaciers, the racket of
helicopters searching for lost
climbers, anything that spoils our
violet reveries with the night.

His hope-coffers are empty.
She doesn't know who he or anyone else
is. She thrashes wall to wall like
a trapped bird. No one wants to help
him take care of her—the waiting lists
at the facilities up to a year.
I need something, she tells him, *but
I can't tell you what it is.*

She hasn't slept for days.
The medicine that opens the sleep door
doesn't work on her. The anti-psychotics
don't tamp down the fear anymore.
She's like watching a lightning storm
over a lake, doubled and single-minded

at once. No comforting arms
for her. She won't be placated. She's
a force now, like wind or rip tide,
uttering unanswerable edicts as it
dashes things to pieces. He dashes
each suggestion I make. Too late
for that. Or that.

Now we know why the old women
are lighting candles in the dark alcove
of the church, kindling a wavering city
of light, white candle burning next to white
candle. Maybe that's the trace hope leaves
when it's emptied out by crude events—reduced
to a sign, a silent cry made of light.

for Greg

In Lilac-Light

That's what poems are for,
unlivable love.

NOTEBOOK ENTRY

She is so eager for any emerging
sign of spring, she cuts the stems in bud,
tight seeds before scent that will push open
four-pronged lavender fists,
what she makes visible of her deep will
to live. She places them like the bowed heads
of sea horses in the glass pitcher *to drink*
while we talk.

The mystery novel someone loaned
lies unread on the table. And why not?
She lives the more-than-mystery
of last days. Time-gone, like giddy
mountain air, has expanded her gaze—its
great stillness, its focus
without center.

Scent of lilacs to come.
Scent of lemon and coriander
from the meal I've carried to her
in the cast-iron skillet. She lights
the swirled golden candlestick
given by an enemy, yet saved
for a special occasion. All are
special now. Its flame leaps to air.
In lilac-light even enemies
grow benign.

Hooves strike long sparks
on the cobblestones of memory.
She talks about Margie, the little gray mare
she rode to school through snow seventy
and more years ago. "Give me a horse today,
I could ride it!" she says.

How air-blue we are with dusk
coming on, the Celtic whisper—*duskus*
Josie names it, so we embody the *us* of dusk,
plea and surrender, to which we are
a violet inner chamber.

My mother steps through a doorway
in Leadmine, Missouri—lilacs
in her hands, where my young father,
celebrating his birthday, sees a woman
whose waist-length hair sweeps the room
so he must ask, as in a fable,
Who is that black-haired woman?
He does not look away from where she
stands and stands the rest of his lifetime,
holding to the singe of their locked embrace,
its blackened rim of purpose, of room-dulled passion
whose release I am.

Dusk, papery husk of night
before night, let me have one wish
on the brink of a speaking silence: not
to betray their story which, like the scent

of lilacs, comes from outside itself, the lie and lack
so unerringly mixed, daughter and mother are
one breath, descending into this gradual
over-sweet eviction.

WITH SETOUCHI-SAN IN KYŌTO

We are like two sisters separated at birth.
We giggle with delight in each other's presence.
After a while we turn to talk
of love so perfected that when the husband dies
it isolates. But I've gone on nonetheless
to love again. Setouchi-san
explains the plight of widows
in Japan whose families bury them
alive, for they cannot begin anew.

The tape recorder is on. Our words
are like distant rain. *One cannot mourn*
forever, even when one mourns
forever. The heart finds a chink
in the dark. I give her my late love
as example, permission.
If one widow brightens,
a cosmos ignites.

Setouchi-san's belief in love
is my passport. We lock
little fingers, sealing a promise
that next time she'll come to me.
We know the odds
are against it. But even vows
that can't be enacted are important.
Her fervent wish spires
the moment. After long illness, easy
to think we may never see
each other again.

But fervency says otherwise,
says: *this side, or that.*

for Setouchi-san, for Hiromi

SIXTEENTH ANNIVERSARY

You died early and in summer.

Today, observing the anniversary
in a cabin at La Push,
I wandered down to the gray-shingled
schoolhouse at the edge of the sea.
A Quileute carver came out of a low shed.
He held classes in there, he said. Six
students at a time. He taught me
how to say *"I'm going home"*
in Quileute by holding my tongue in
one side of my cheek,
letting the sounds slur past it, air
from the far cheek
a kind of bellows.

I felt an entirely other
spirit enter my body. It
made a shiver rise up in me
and I said so. The carver
nodded and smiled. He
said he taught carving
while speaking Quileute.
I imagined that affected
the outcome, for the syllables
compelled a breath in me
I'd never experienced before.

He showed me a rattle
in the shape of a killer whale
he'd been carving. The tail

had split off, but he said he
could glue it back. He let me
shake it while he sang
a rowing song they used
when whaling. My whole arm
disappeared into the song;
the small stones inside
the whale kept pelting
the universe, the sound
raying out into the past
and future at once,
never leaving the moment.

He told me his Quileute name,
which he said didn't mean
anything except those syllables.
Just a name. But I knew he
preferred it to any other. "I'm going
home," I said, the best I could
in his language, when
it was time to walk on
down the beach. Fog
was rolling in so the rocks
offshore began to look
conspiratorial. He offered
his hand to shake. Our
agreement, what was it?
Wordless. Like what
the fog says when it
swallows up an ocean.
He swallowed me up

and I swallowed him up.
And we felt good about it.

You died early and in summer.

Before heading to the cemetery
I made them leave the lid up
while I ran out to the garden
and picked one more bouquet
of sweet peas to fan onto your
chest, remembering how you
beamed when I placed them
on your writing desk in
the mornings. You'd draw
the scent in deeply,
then I'd kiss you on the brow,
go out, and quietly close
the door.

We survive on ritual, on
sweet peas in August, letting
the scent carry us, so at last the door
swings open and we're both
on the same side of it
for a while.

If you were here we'd
sit outside, accompanying
the roar of waves
as they mingle with the low notes
of the buoy bell's plaintive warning,

like some child blowing
against the cold edge of a metal pipe.
I'd tell you how the Quileute
were transformed from wolves
into people, though I'm unsure
if they liked the change. I'm
not the same myself, since
their language came into me.
I see things differently.
With a wolf gazing out.
I can't help my changes any more
than you could yours. Our life apart
has outstripped the mute kaleidoscope
of the hydrangea and its seven changes.
I'm looking for
the moon now. We'll have
something new
to say to each other.

August 2, 2004
for Raymond Carver
and for Chris Morgenroth,
Quileute Nation

What the New Day Is For

The marvel of day after night, after
sleep-travel in one place, after stretching
the body out—its surrender.
The marvel that sleep is not
the quicksand it seems
to the child, that the raft of it
carries us into morning, and that
whatever made us weep yesterday
has been strangely visited without us
and, its terms, though unrelentingly
the same, lift our night-changed hearts.

The new day has been given
so whatever befell us yesterday
can be withstood, not as it was,
but as if we had perished
into it, and, despite horror or joy,
something miraculous could be
done with us that surpasses even hope,
which only wants ascension of the prospect
and not the helpless, dire turn—its
clang and echo.

As the carriage horse
waits for the child's hand on its nose
or flank, memory awaits the new day,
wants to be stroked—to marvel that
with no engine except blood and bone or
a wondrous toss of mane and forelock—
the fable of the freshly given day
can carry not only itself, but

all those other days
that caused a horse and open carriage
to stand for what we remember
of the past in our midst.

So the new day in our presence is given
to pass unforgetting hands
before twin tunnels of breath flowing
through the horse's nostrils, sweet and warm
from a great moving oven that insists
that the dough rise, that somehow the hungry
be fed, and that a lost child, when it is
found living, despite the cold
of the mountain, assuages
as a balm and an abiding
beyond even the new day.

Not because a child
is so wonderful—whining and helpless and
freighted with unanswerable mother-love, but
because for reasons we don't stop
to understand, we have more mercy
for the child than the world has.
And we know this. For such knowing
makes spirits of us, sends the new day,
before which we are again ourselves,
and more. Having flickered against dread
we rise afresh, recomposed
by the many-chambered parameters
of the night releasing us.

Snow falls onto the lashes
of the carriage horse. Slow dark orbs
in their frosted caves of sight
stare down the wounds
of mere bodies, coax us out
as apparitions: what the new day
is for.

for Jiri, Lenka, Alice, and Agata
in Prague

COMEBACK

My father loved first light.
He would sit alone
at the yellow Formica table
in the kitchen with his coffee cup
and sip and look out
over the strait. I too
am addicted to slow sweet beginnings.
First bird call. Wings
in silhouette. How the steeples
of the evergreens make a selvage
for the gaunt emerging sky.

My three loves are far away
in other countries,
and one is even under
this dew-bright ground
where the little herds
of jittery quail peck
and scurry for their lives.

My father picks up his
cup. Light is sifting in
like a gloam of certainty
over the water. He knows
something there in the half-light
he can't know any other way.

And now I know it with him: so much
is joining us in the dawn
that no one can ever be parted.
It steals over us because we left

the warm beds of our dreams
to sit beside what rises.
I think he wants to stay there
forever, my captain, gazing but not
expecting, while the world
begins, and, in a stark silent calling,
won't tell anyone what it's for.

DEATH'S INK

like petroleum or toothpaste, comes
in viscous suspensions, watery seepage,
or the fatefully indelible.
A serious, too serious poet tried to fill the pen
as often as possible from its rollicking vein.
For like a heft of sea in calm, we bless
ourselves in knowing what's under us,
that it is deep and cold and uncontrollable.

A young poet, far from death, I wanted
to scrawl green ink over all that happened,
as if to inoculate the future.
When friends died, I ran to memory
like a second mother, shoring up
with a blurry nib a glimpse, some jaunty
cock of hat or squint into light on water.

What my father said one day
when we were driving: *I've broken every bone
in my body.* I wrote that down on the back
of a water bill. Also the story Keiko
told of orphaned Japanese babies
handed over to the Chinese to save, wrapped
in moss-blue silk or wearing some handmade
garment, no other sign of where they'd come from.

Fifty years they clung to the shreds of their
swaddling clothes like identity cards,
still searching for their parents.
This too, saved with death's ink, because death
is the haven of hapless searchings—lost babes,

lost fathers and mothers, the washed-out ink
of their names that leaves them invisibly written
into time, as it runs out, and the valiance
of the search is all that's left, or the pen
scratching the tree inside the paper
to emboss moonlight on forest ferns
or on the snowy vault
of Mt. Olympus—the eyelet step

of a deer. Ink that is a laceration
in the dream of morning, our waking
to sunlight glinting offshore of the mind.
Ink I follow like a trail of bird song,
stepping over dead soldiers, over
entire kingdoms, over stars
dead or waiting to be quenched.
For only with death's eggshell nimbus
around each word could I break through
life's greedy confinement and discover
the impudent clot each period insinuates,
a rest stop for death, holding back syntax

until meaning catches up.
Until the babes cross the border of
held-back-time and a swatch of cloth
brightens memory's jaguar eye. Nothing
matches the undiscovered embrace
of those who remain unrecognized.
Death's ink loves them more. And my father's
broken bones are mended underground
because I recall his handsome swagger, his skill

at cards, his fearless venturing to top a tree
eighty feet from earth. I loan to life
this blooded ink that agrees to pass out of time
without loss or memory, having given over in tatters
the spirit I ransacked like a despot.
So the period falls with a clang.
And all goes on—

Signature

New Poems
2011

> *"The earth has been thought to be flat . . . science has proved that the earth is round . . . they persist nowadays in believing that life is flat and runs from birth to death. However, life, too, is probably round."*

VINCENT VAN GOGH

RED PERCH

> *But for the red perch in the black stream*
> *my life has been nothing . . .*
>
> PAUL DURCAN

Low fog-bloom of morning across the islands
of Lough Arrow below Carrowkeel
and the passage graves. I'm full circle
to my runaway coach of the sixties,
a rented caravan parked near Abbey Ballindoon
to write poems, and Yvonne, just twelve,
coming faithfully on her bicycle to bring
tea and her clarified heart, a listening
I can still touch these forty years hence.
"Oh, keep it!" she'd plead for a poem
I was throwing out, as if it were a stray cat
needing shelter. More than mercy
how poems moved her. Every young poet
should wish for such a listener, a bare
and eager companion to trance. What she

must have thought, neighboring war-grief,
my young pilot husband strafing
in Vietnam and no way to compass the unseen
damage. "But for the red perch in the black
stream . . ." and she, asking questions
about love and death and friendship.
Her life cut short by cancer
a year after she'd married
so she's come to rest
a few hundred yards from my cottage.

That strange aftermath, her letter
discovered after her death,
telling me in first glow
she had met her love. The great luck accomplished,
she wanted me to know.
Red perch, red perch, it has all been
a remaking in the black stream.

There is a coal tit that pecks every morning
at my windows until I come.
It's her, I think, wanting in.
Her favorite uncle, Josie, my own love,
gives the thought a chance
and when, day after day, the bird returns,
we don't call her name, but
like air after flight,
she is there.

for Yvonne McDonagh-Gaffney

SRUTHLINN SPRING

Sent as children to gather watercress
on the lake side of the abbey
where water sprang from ground, its
ice-darkened charge of minerals
with cleansing bite of watercress
the water had riffled through
on its way from darkness into light.

A handful of oats thrown into a well
at North Barroe reappeared
two miles away at *Sruthlinn*—proof
of secret journeying. I drank its water
before it reached the abbey, pulled
150 feet up from Eileen Frazier's well
in 1968, the bright gong of it
in the mouth. Yvonne and I made tea
with it, talking poetry
near Ballindoon graveyard
in Tommy Flynn's caravan.

This spring so rainless we think:
"summer of '69" to savor the rarity—spring
of unstoppable sunshine, a stretch
of goldfinch mornings.
I walk past names of two I treasure
on a quiet mission of again finding
watercress, brushed by the cool
underground of presence, and
as mind will—going in one place,
coming out another.

MAURICE'S FOAL

Seeing that mare across a field,
head up, tail at flare, a prancing
trot, was to glimpse beauty not
watching itself. He sold her
nonetheless, then had to buy her
back. Now she's given him
something for his trouble—a brown
and white skewbald foal.

On the under lip a candle-run of pink
makes the new head seem to be
sticking out its tongue. He offers
no fear of me while the mare
churns ground, glares walleyed.
He tries the back of my hand for clues,
his touch a bumblebee fumbling
a doorknob, the nothing-to-eat

of me. Maurice, having watched
any number of foals get up
a first time, says the hardest
thing is their figuring how to lie
down—the cranky folding up of
a lawn chair by an exhausted child
at lakeside after the adults have strolled
the picnic blanket away. He is

a puzzle of himself, the not-him
of himself. That quickly
he tumbles, then rearranges
the bony heap where it has abandoned

him, muzzle against the grass. Easy
to think we do it all in this perilous
life until, slammed down, we crash
into ourselves where the weeping
child drags a slab of wood that was a chair

across a field and the parents don't
look back—or this foal unfolds itself,
bows its fringed neck to its kindling-sprawl
and so-whats itself, un-legs itself against earth
that was not even earth, but
some accomplished falling
that came over him.

PERISHED

Not waving but drowning.

STEVIE SMITH

One minute they were laughing,
the next they were drowning, four
young men elated with their catch.

Had they not been tempted, had they not
pulled their skiff ashore
at Ballinafad and indulged too freely,
the trout would have made the pan.
As it was, dead trout and live men
went into Lough Arrow, and only
dead men came out.

One minute they were laughing,
the next they were drowning.

Three of them farmers, and Charlton
slated for good-byes to America.
But he made no good-byes and never would be
found, for the lake takes a drink
any way it can, and four good men, careless
on a Sabbath make a party.

It was cold that day and fair.
One minute they were laughing,
the next they were drowning.

Had it not been the Sabbath, had
there been no pubs in Ballinafad, had

they caught no trout, all might have been well
and Charlton gone to America
with good leave taken.

One minute they were laughing,
the next they were drowning and soon
the fishing was for men.

The lake kept one of the four in 1848
to cry on foul nights, to laugh
and to linger far from shore, as if
a death now and then is needed
to freshen and sustain
all unsaid good-byes.

When the lake is wild, laughter
can be heard from Charlton, bound
for America, washed by river currents
under continents, pulling him
this way and that.

One minute they were laughing,
the next they were drowning.

Charlton alone floats deep, folded in
and under with companions all merry,
those farmers who went home to land, as he
stayed endless with water, transformed
by the general mind of all who carry him now
as a voice inside the wind.

Horse Dealers

I'm speaking like a mother
in my silk voice to the new foal
but am warned off. The man says
the book says not to get cozy
or the horse won't jump.
I whisper to the foal, "Your eyes
are stamped with moonbeams
and midnight grass."

He loves this strange silk
and if I wished
would stand under my hand
all morning, his muzzle so
prickly velvet. What a nice penalty
for disobedience.

My first horse
pushed his nose into my armpit
to drink in my scent.
Man O' War, after his last race,
nuzzling his groom's pocket
for one cube of sugar.

BALLERINA

Comes Mickey Moran, his arm thrust
like a battering ram against the sky; no
greeting in the world so accomplished—half
adoration, half astonishment and
three-quarters mock submission.
I know I'm home when he clatters by
on his tractor, never failing to spot me
going or coming, rising out of a hedge,
his bounty worth crossing an ocean. Pity
at home in Ameri-*kay* how they put
their heads down between their shoulders
like sick vultures on a stobby limb
and don't look up.

But my recognition is a knighthood here—
and I swear, this smile and wave are your match,
Mickey Moran, midwife of sheep and calves and foals
to all of Ballindoon, and us reborn thrice a day
in greetings. Or is it good-byes in our white heads
and hearts still backward enough
for romantic love that is all inclination and no loss
of virtue, me under my parasol, you
in your sexy red cab shuddering
towards the crossroad?

BRUSHING FATE

On the road from Ballindoon, night
of no moon, haze-your-breath night,
driving the hedge-high gauze of turns
like plunging eyes-first
down a wormhole. Sudden silvery slump
of badger caught in headlight magnification
by which night diminishes
and badger looms.

How I need you, badger, so the world
can again be strange enough
to save. Beautiful forlorn of winter,
and Josie's foot down hard
on the brake. Badger does not so much
as glance, as if his errand in the night could not
have been broken by any force, its current so strong,
bearing him and us
away from that hollowed-out

moment, cave-of-never in which life is
everlasting and renewed by simply going on
past averted calamity. Our late night meal
of potatoes, fish and cauliflower
tasting better because badger did not die.
The night younger too, sitting by coal fire
in the cottage overlooking Lough Arrow, me
trying to explain, because Josie asks, the ruin
of young love by war, my first husband
having come home some-sort-of-alive
from Vietnam thirty years ago,

carrying in his pocket shrapnel dislodged
from his plane, memento of one fate
having spared him
so another could put him down.
He was made use of, as we do
make use, and are forever shamed and stupid and young,
until night gets smaller, illuminating
two figures—a man, a woman,
whose one-time embrace still has the power
to brush hearts past midnight,
as if we'd saved them a little
to be in love ourselves, and worse than war
careening the darkness, worse
than death and forgetting
about to come toward
us. In that loophole moment

badger let us have again the freezing stars
of an Irish morning. Only in that slip-knot time
of near-miss could those we are torn from
loom again, and in the starkness
of lost love, could you see me
afresh, Josie, and hesitate crucially
for him you never knew.

for Lawrence Gallagher and Josie Gray

Lie Down with the Lamb

and rise with the bird—
an old Irish saying meant to keep
the riverbank of the day: David's lambs
are grazing the lush green
of Ballindoon, green fortified
with limestone. When the man
is late a week to carry them
to market, I decide to save one.
For eighty euro I buy her back
from the slaughterhouse. *She
is white with a black head,*
Josie writes, *and sixteen mothers
are looking after her.* While
my country makes war, one lamb
is saved in the West of Ireland,
a sign to what oppresses, but a sign
of what? That in helplessness before
atrocities any innocence is oasis?

I drink from you, my lamb,
although I have never seen you.
But hearing they held you back,
how account for the white funnel
of joy you make on a bank of green
for no one's sake? My dusk
lies down with you a continent,
an ocean away. You are my army
of one, though your brothers and sisters
are gone to table. So are we all
bought and sold in the coin of the realm.

Lie down, my lamb, with the piteous
cries of your mothers. You are saved,
as surely as the bird will rise.
Saved and with no use
except to run free on a hillside,
peaceful and far from the horrors
of war, where sacrifice is shamed
by terms other than its own
pure gift. Lamb, I wish it were
otherwise, and my wish
is your life.
I've done the next-to-nothing I could.
As surely as that, we rise
with the bird.

Eyelets

Tess: *What if a man appeared at our bedroom window?*
Josie: *I'd ask for help.*

~

Tess: *You talk a lot about horses.*
Josie: *If you could shite walking you'd be all right.*

~

Tess: *Are you listening?*
Josie: *You have to listen to thunder.*

~

Tess: *We'll need a plunger.*
Josie: *Might need more than that.*
Tess: *Did you ever hear of a "snake?"*
Josie: *Only the one sitting beside me.*

~

Passing a waterfall at the side of the road.
Josie: *Look at the horse's tail!*

~

Tess: *How do the new shoes fit?*
Josie: *I'll have to wear them awhile before I put them on.*

~

Tess: *Why is that moon always standing in my doorway?*
Josie: *Because it has no real respect!*

SMALL AND INDESTRUCTIBLE

Her fingers, harmed
with arthritis, hinge
to the cup handle
like a backward wing.
A ruff of brown-red fur
tufts each wrist, cloaks
the neck. She and her
lady-friend are fully engaged,
having tea at the bakery
in their village—Virginia, near
Cavan. Her hat queens her
in the swirl of home-going
bread-buyers. Like a plover
on its nest, she adjusts herself
to her chair. It is plain
she cannot rise to flight, but
like a bee inside a foxglove,
she has nuzzled out
something sweet from life
and is sharing it in this
sustained intimacy abroad
with the multitudes. We,
who take more than strength
from her, buy our loaf
and go.

for Sheila Gray

JEALOUS

He says his wife is jealous
of a woman who used to be
a waitress. He admits she's
left employ and he has to go to
her house to do the crossword,
at great inconvenience, mind
you, but something they
enjoyed doing together at
the restaurant those mornings
she brought him coffee
while his wife was at work.
"For godsake, it's only
the crossword," he pleads,
though I've said nothing.
He's come to gather leaves
and rake gravel into potholes
down the driveway.

Last night he witnessed his wife
carrying all the pillows in the house
into the living room to make beds
for her family. They'd finally come
home, she believed, and needed
a soft place to sleep. Only trouble,
there was no one there, only
himself. He missed the next day
at the leaves. When I inquired,
it was bronchitis. He often had
bronchitis. "Someone," he said, phoned
for the wife and, tired of lying,
he heard himself say, "She's

passed out in bed. I don't know when
she's getting up."

The morning after the pillow
encampment he checked her into
Emergency where she was released
to him with medication to counteract
hallucinations. She'd been in detox
three times, he revealed, and his tone
said he'd had it. *But a waitress.*
A crossword puzzle.
Not even sex. Surely his wife
had to be kidding.

I studied the riddle with him briefly,
then, handing him the rake,
said the mysterious word aloud:
intimacy. "Oh," he said,
pulling stones into a small socket
of rain-filled space
between us.

CONTRABAND

"He'll always be bringing home
some old drunk, or fool," she said.
My father woke me: "get up, put on
your coat"—the fire out in the stove.
My brothers left sleeping.

Scarves, multicolored silk, threaded
through my ears, the head
nothing but a corridor for marvels.
A deck of cards arched accordion style
overhead, then collapsed to a single ace
plucked from my brow. But when the white dove
took wing from his black silk hat

something else opened
in the room: my former sleeping self
sat upright, as at some verge between worlds.
The dove fumbled the piano keyboard
then landed fugitive, high on the wall
near the toy violin, to stare incredulously down
on us like a fierce red-eyed god.

I never gave a thought to the rest
of that bird's life, flown free
this lifetime since—a father's gift
to his sleeping child.

But showing the stranger
out that night, we stood with cold
and stars—my father's work-thickened hand

in mine, and like a dove concealed:
the long, stumbling good-bye of thanks
he gave that borrowed magician
for more than my sake.

Mr. and Mrs. Rat

behind the cottage, stealing in daylight
from the bird feeder. Josie
is not amused. Soon I don't
see them anymore.
Months later I come across
rat poison under
a flower pot and learn
their fate. From bonanza
to the last gate.

ABANDONED LUNCH

Fresh pineapple in shredded carrots
juiced with lemon. Boiled red potatoes.
Smoked salmon with capers and rocket.
Seven hours and no one appears to eat.
A friend comes. We sit in sunshine and notice
the swallows are back. Someone had said
only yesterday: "Where are the swallows?"
News of mute swans congregating
on the lake near Tommy Flynn's pier.

At Kilronan Castle a bride, before
four hundred guests, when asked,
"Do you take," says *No*. Imagining the drink
must still have been drunk, the cake
eaten. Or maybe not. Conjecture then
as to why such an apex before witnesses—
something cruel after discovery? Or was it
fear unreasoning the instant? Chances
are she did not know herself the javelin

she'd pitch. We agree it all had to be
paid for, right down to the Italian lace
and the something blue she would take off
later with the something old, and the rollicking
new that stretched out before her with vistas
of the sea she could not quite pull into
focus as she relinquished her bouquet like
someone passing a butter knife. Cancellations
in a flock—no limousine, no honeymoon
cruise, no toasting to their missed Forever.

What a bright day we're having, soaking in
Irish sun which astonishes like no other
for all its missed occasions. Alone later,
perhaps, with her mother, all would be swept
away as "for the better." We decide to climb

the bank to cut briars as the lunch sags
on the counter. Soon the appetites can be
heard rattling pans in the kitchen. But we don't
descend for salvage. "I'd say she was happy,"
my friend muses. We smile, looking out
toward Bricklieve, one of us
"still looking," we who know nothing about life.

A Fozy Bog

Fozy is not *foosie,* said the Irish schoolmaster.
French toast could be called *fozy,* springy
yet able to absorb. *Foosie* meant bitchy. "She
was *foosie* in front of his friends."

He knew things and would tell
you: "Trees migrate, sit out change
or go extinct. Trees on remote islands
cannot migrate." But the story he loved most
was of Darwin who killed the *chilla* fox
by striking it a blow on the head with a hammer
while it was "intently watching the crew
of the *Beagle.*" Notoriously unwary, it
was unable to realize it should run
from humans.

Red fox, you are sunk into the *fozy*
of my brain. I was unwary and am sinking
with you now—two unwaries suspended
by engulfment. Even if we exchange
identities we won't avoid the hammer,
the sinking, the wistfulness of others
that we had been less curious, less drawn
by what we did not understand or what
fascinated, as strangeness does.

I will never comprehend that hammer.
Nor all those collections accomplished by
hammer-rectitude upon the unwary.
Unwary women, unwary foxes, unwary
bogs. Curl up, little fox. We have a long sleep

coming to us among the bones of the Celts.
Our island migration by way of stillness
and laying on of earth
is just beginning.

Barrie Cooke Painting

I who am usually a verb looking for its subject
am his subject. Still, I have no trouble
sitting still, asking permission to leave
my body, to which he assents, having no need
of anything so crass as personality
or spiritual innuendo.

"For me you will be simply landscape,"
he says, coaxing me to abandon hope
of influencing what will be done with me,
my ravines and alcoves, my hillocks
and dales, my ruddy chapters, former
husbands and the like.

Now he is squinting like a man with his nose
in a tourniquet and dancing backwards
from the one appearing next to me.
Then, extending his brush as a sighting tool,
he rushes forward to adjust the spatial
equanimity of she to whom I am
but reference, in the time to time of glance.

The delicious sensation of skidding about
in the elsewhere of the artist's
pirouetting to and fro towards one's surrogate,
while freely and gleefully I do roam
in the out and away, the updraft
of what a field must feel when a black horse
with a white blaze lies down full
in sun to have a soak. But no, he has disrupted

me, brought me crashing with a look cold
as spring water in a rill! Oh he would kill, kill, kill
if I had to pee, but I can be said to have taken care
of myself like any good landscape blabbering silently
day in and out to whatever trammels it,
caring not whether beast or bones are flung down
upon it or beauty whispered into it
by some passerby.

For now I can never entirely die. I feel
suddenly more generous like sky shut down
by stars—why shouldn't I make do
in this complexity of self-abnegation,
the way a tree can be said to take shelter
when pelted with birds on the way
to somewhere else. Else how would posterity
and one's posterior ever be brought
to dialogue without this *interminable*—which,

through an alchemy of my gullies
and enchanted valleys, I am subduing entirely,
or almost, for the sake of art.
Whereupon I bash his reverie of do-si-do
with "the figure" to muse aloud on Modigliani
blanking the eyes in his portraits—as if
forcing the birdness of being into impenetrable
retreat by discarding essence, a sacrifice
to autonomy which a gaze could only interrupt.

At our second session he is deciding not
to paint me with hair. He confesses he got up
in the night to try hair, but the fizzog would not
accept fringing. Lucky for him I am intimate
with my pate and prefer it, allowing an unruly
hedge simply to take the scare out of things.
Meanwhile I have talked too much
and he has rubbed out the eyes, which I well
deserved. But whilst he mulls aloud
the sexuality of painting nudes, he is canny
to work the orbs back in and does not rest until
the sun and moon are restored to my firmament.

We both take a look at her with a deep
conjoined curiosity, at how I can be two places
at once, and my *not-at-all* insinuating itself
like a cryptic quatrain by Nostradamus.
I am mild and melancholy as a mate-less
swan at midnight in my black ruff,
perfectly executed, both moderne and
Elizabethan to his brush.

Then like two lost children on a bridge
in a rainstorm we give each other a hug,
a right punctuation when words to this endowment
would be mere landscape. Just to make sure
I can walk away, I remind him of that boiled egg
he promised me for lunch.

As I warned, I am usually and preferably a verb,
though something still and ruthlessly
beyond me will be that gazing each of us sheds
in avalanche to look away from *her.*

As for me, I'll take away
Barrie dancing.

Irish Weather

Rain squalls cast sideways,
the droplets visible
like wheat grains
sprayed from the combine.
As suddenly, sunshine.
If a person behaved
this way we'd call them
neurotic. Given weather, we gust
and plunder with only
small comment: it's
raining; sun's out.

WALKING ON ANNAUGH LOY

Two snails a yardstick apart
scale the Everest of my cottage
at Ballindoon while I walk the road
past Lady Kingston's, former
hunting lodge of the Rockingham gentry,
sold now to a handsome couple
who garland the gates with strong locks
and chains, and who appear at intervals.
My walking partner and I are up and
over with a borrowed collie
from neighbor Hargadon's.

Rowboats wait for mayflies
near the locked boat house. On the lake
two swans float by like wedding cakes.
What are these plants whose wrist-thick stalks
run a canopy of elephant ears over our embarrassing
perambulation, intersected now by an Irish
setter who cavorts with the collie into
the blue hydrangea? Delicious to think:
we are caught out in wishful snooping,
skewered by owners returned to their
rightful ground. But no, we are at liberty

to imagine cricket on the lawn, a harp of roses
strummed by wind clinging to the lordly
manor. A wishing well or cistern seems
abandoned, but neither of us has a coin
for drowning. Back over the gate to stroll
with Lough Arrow to either side.
Our conversation calls up Josie's self-deprecating

humor: "Oh *him*. He wouldn't give you the frost
off his pee!"—teasing that he, as my good neighbor,
should not be relied on for matches.

My friend and I talk news: a government eviction
of men in rehabilitation, lives once turned
to the good, suddenly loosed again
to old choices: prison, drugs or suicide.
The peace of this place is a magnet
to disruptions, so unlike the noiseless ascent
of snails clinging to my ridge slates above
Saint Dominick's rock, tempting
the cliff's edge of my roof. Beyond the brow
of Jimmy Frazier's field lies Ballindoon graveyard,

which they must see as encampments of giants
where the living trespass with their eruptive
offerings of flowers and candles.
But perhaps the pair, having rappelled the eaves
and attained a promontory, is inside
lighting celebratory lanterns, their mortgage-free
shelter secured for the night. Orion dangles blue Rijl
over them into morning. I think they have affected
my dreams—that bride who is clearly
a corpse but still asks for help getting into
her wedding dress.

By morning they have quit the place, foraging
among winter pansies. Enlarged by their daring
and self-sufficiency, I can't get them out
of my head. When I discover one skirting accidental hell

along the fireplace mantel, I enact
a giant's beneficence, transporting it, antlers twitching,
onto the hedge to join others of its admirable kind.

Since snails got into my head
I am sleeping somewhere dark under bridges,
and neither rain nor stars gleam romantic.
For snails have, no doubt, had hard lessons
from an inhospitable world. Thus
those houses that are their backs.

SMALL HUT

I know you only in echo,
as your parents confide—the wound of it
borne as if grief were life's only message
when you have one son
who takes his life
from his life, their lives.

Your mother says she can't see you
past your knees. Hard to know you as *you*
in your afterlife where she tries to follow
in mind to see are you all right there.
She feels cheated, unable
to see your face which
you obliterated, taking yourself
out of here.

You'd tried before, then promised
to get help, go to AA, find
a sponsor; and you meant to, but
for reasons you kept from them,
and maybe even from yourself,
could not. We lose humanity
if we miss knowing
the full range of choices
that might have led you from harm
did not open to you in that deadly hour.

With non-specific pain
all doorways must seem very specifically
shut. We sit together with your "maybes"
which outlive you. Those who love you

are stuffing you with intensions.
The good woman who left you, she
left just in time not to be
the assumed reason
you succeeded this time in putting the world
to sleep.

Hearing on Irish radio of another man whose son
was beaten to death, then thrown
onto the railroad tracks when the murderer
wanted to hide his deed—how that father knew
where the unconvicted killer lived and would stand
at intervals in the night before the house
and howl: *You murderer! You*
killed my son! over and over,

I wish I could build a small hut, a wailing hut
where your father could stand similarly and cry
against the facelessness of loss incubating its "whys."
And even if the killer never comes out
to face his accusers, it's a brand
on the communal heart to have one father cry like that
with his whole being,
trying to make a rectitude with only his voice
and his love raking the night.

If the door of this hut opened, and
the murderer stepped out, it would be easier
to see this was not your son, and the grief
would bear two forms—the desperate one

who took him, and the one we love
when love asks everything.

But did the father go home?
He went home.

What did he there?
He sat with his wife and they drank together
peppermint tea, calming themselves.
They had to make dinner.
They had to see to things.

But beyond that
they found themselves in love in an entirely
new unspeakable way
with each other
and with their ever prodigal son.

>   *for Russell Guthrie*
>   *and his parents, Ann and Jim*

Between the Voice and the Feather

for Edith Piaf

Her voice-pulse gouges its echo of presence
against a dark rim of shore.

A voice with its hands on its hips.
Not the cliché of wreckage and salvage, but
the lightness of one feather without
its bird-proof. Restorative power of song
cleansed of regret. Especially
the song recalled from childhood, that lost ocean.

Memory of oceans; the Atlantic at Strandhill
mixes with the Pacific at La Push—milky, luminous
mind-stream tossed toward a vast inner feasting,
its meld of gypsy-oblivion, of raw exhalation, the sea
withdrawing so as to dash up with force.

The bee of sorrow had stung her heart, until
there was no such thing as listening. Hearing
takes up its own body, as when the spirit
craves to empty out, to rouse its pains at a rough pitch
that refuses to be entirely soothed away.

What was her courage except a buoyancy
where sorrow coexists with joy—her jaunty
flaunting of extremes?

The gaze of her voice fixed on something far away.
The bee of sorrow had stung her heart.

SIGNATURE

Take a photograph of a tree, initials
carved into it, near a makeshift dock
at the lake edge. But when he asks why,
the telephone goes quiet, then
a father tumbled out of himself, unable
for words, which fumble and braille:
a son and daughter on the lake with him, one

of those days Eden-made in the moment,
of looking out as an *into,* a joy-dissolving
beauty where even joy would be disruption.
Amplification only possible in the silent
companioning of his children—the boy
late teens, she younger. Just the day before,
a walk together in brilliant weather up Croagh Patrick.

The father and children walking where
they would always walk in the mind
of the father's remembering, more perfect now
than life could make it, illuminated by loss,
yet more gift than loss. The photographer
listened, took down the tree's location and,
with his own son, struck out on foot
toward the lake to find it.
He had not asked how the son had died
two years after the knife tip scraped channels
into bark, asking a step too far when grief

was bare, like coming upon birds' eggs in a nest
and knowing not to touch.
Finding then, marks driven to clarity

by the boy, talisman to what we call *being here,*
and he had been. Some shard of motion, of moment,
of pressing against the dream of being bodied
had entered the space now held by the tree,
and the message of two perfect days revisited
by that marking-intention of children, one

alive, one not—a father could cling to this,
thinking how much worse without the sign,
the emblem of the names given them
at birth. It was dark under the tree.
The photographer hated to disturb the place
with a flash. Turning the speed up then, opening
the lens toward the click. His own hand,
as if it had been underground, finding
his son's shoulder as they walked out again,
held by the reverberative membrane of love.

for Brian and Eddie

TIERNAN AT FIVE

He's figuring it out
in the backseat of the car
on the way to the ferry.
"But Teeta, what if you die
before I can see you again, then
I'll never see you again?" He's so
sincere I nearly believe
I'll die—but no, for him alone
I am suddenly immortal. "Don't
worry, darling. I'm not going to, never
going to die."

We ride the lie to the dock
where he cries, bereft for us both,
waving me out of sight.
And my own eyes
dry as a stick, though for him
I am dying and he may never
see me again—old woman who shot
marbles with him in the driveway, who
pleaded with the Red Riding Hood wolf
not to be eaten, while he ate her
for delight, and now sailing away
with a useless arm.
Then gone.
The quick of it.

Karver Bookstore: Montenegro

After my poems, read in translation
by Varja against a backdrop of photos
projected of Ray and me when we were young,
the man in the black leather jacket
approaches to tell me he hates the Irish,
especially the sound of their language.
I repeat that I am Irish, Cherokee and English,
something already mentioned in Varja's
introduction. He doesn't register.
He worked with an Irishman. He now *knows*
all Irish people. Nonetheless he pursues me

at the party. Having heard of my cancer
survival, he confesses a fear
of prostate cancer. He wants to know
my treatment, trying to gauge my
survival chances from drug properties—
how much was done to keep me here.
From his questions I realize he's
a pharmaceutical salesman. He casts

a rant against everyone around us who
is smoking and that *is* everyone. "You
could have stopped Ray," he tosses, widening
his will to damage. Not having met Ray's demons
he could imagine lifting
them. Nonetheless, I wish it had been true,
and that Ray was, in fact,
standing there instead of me.

But I cannot even calm this man.
Soon two writers lift him under his arms
and carry him outside like a small disabled

scarecrow. The residue of accusation, of
hating the Irish, of disgust with smokers
hangs in the air—everyone still
talking about him. "He said he was
from Sarajevo," Varja says, "but maybe just
to engage my emotions."
Someone offers: "His accent was Northern or
maybe Bosnian." "Well, it doesn't matter," Varja
answers. "No, it doesn't matter." Someone else
quietly pulls the moment into
focus. It isn't about where he came from or
ethnic identity. He is one man saying

what he says and getting himself kicked out
onto the terrace above the river while everyone
tries to get away from the sludge, the intricate
detritus of what they wanted to feel
about a man nobody knows who came into
their midst with unhappy things
on his mind, and unhappy ways of trying to make
the world carry it, and him. Yes,

we still have to carry him. And even now,
remembering Ray, I make room for the scald
of him, his heedless taunt, the outcast moment

when his hatred-sword was raised over me
and I wished for him, somewhere out there
in the night, the largesse of that one whose gift
had brought us all together.

DESOLATE ROAD

Thin dog trotting next to traffic
in Podgorica. Wild lost dog or dog
who knows exactly how to
survive? My new friends
pacify me when I ask, "Where
will he get water?"—the sun
beating down. "Oh, he'll
find it." Later, driving the switch-
backs of Black Mountain
villages that run out of water
in summer, just when
they are swarming
with tourists, the cool, dry
villages the cities depend
on in the twin suffocations
of stone and heat—scalded cars
carrying like gold
their water.

Eating Yellow

wild flowers
Ljubo Djurkovic picked for me
from Black Mountain, above his
Montenegrin birthplace, Cetinje,
the stems sweetest where
they have clung
to stone.

THE TALLEST MEN IN EUROPE

are from Montenegro. Also
tall women wearing four-inch
spiked heels. No, I don't want
to be a tall woman or a tall
man. Too much bending.
Better a student of reaching.
But ahh—glimpsing the willow
revises me completely.

SITTING AT LORCA'S PIANO

I couldn't play anything
so I spread one hand against
the tusks of the elephants
sacrificed where the tips
of his fingers had rested,
and the way elephants love their dead
came into me. I loved you, Lorca,
like that: the girl inside the woman
whose childhood piano
sat abandoned in the corner
all those years after
she left home.

Your piano wasn't for playing,
anymore than your bed upstairs
was for sleeping. It was a demonstration
of a piano. Was it the one you
crawled into like a grown-up child
when they came for you? To play
would have been to hide in a piano,
so I sat with you there
and let you play a specially carried
silence in me
with the white ink we use
when we have to go out at night
and write something urgent on the moon.

We've been traveling so long, Lorca,
joined at the wrists, and now I can't play
anything for you, even after
a five-hour train ride from Madrid past

interminable olive groves.
Madrid, where you should have stayed,
because they couldn't hide you here, García Lorca,
at the house of your parents.

Sometimes it's our fate to be marooned
for a while with unplayable pianos, until we
come together in a certain useless dirge
that refreshes us, and we step outside
to compose something zany and out of reach
on the great black piano of the night sky,
something called "Boogie Woogie for Two"
or "Starry Tambourine."

And no one can ever make us play
those dead pianos we needed
to leave behind, not even here, Lorca,
where it was enough to sit—two poets, one
silent piano—until
you lifted my arm by the wrist
and led me away.

A Dusky Glow at Glenstaughey

Hefting turf onto the cart
in the long light, Helen's son Ricardo
gone home. Sufficiency of women's arms
in that old necessity of wars and rain. Mary
stacking the load as we swing the sacks up—good
use of knees to boost the heavier ones
into place. The air still and
brackish, pulling us close
on the hillside. Angela, forgetful in her
silk blouse, brought to the work
so suddenly her white is magnet to the scuff
of earth, the heels of her palms, like ours, etched
with the fine black of secret fire
the earth had been saving.

We ride the bonfire to the cottage yard
to stack the winter's heat. The flickering red
of cockscombs yet to bloom brushes the tractor wheels
to either side. How light
the earth is between us. Strange we are
in the blue air that stores its night.
Strange, like figures crowded off the edge
of memory.

for Mebdh

ABBEY BALLINDOON

Roofless, the abbey crumbles,
yet holds. Mossy stairs ascend
an exterior wall where monks climbed
under stars to their cells.
Coming with Eileen's children
when Vietnamese monks burned
themselves alive, trying to stop a war.

The transfer of bodily grief
over time—our fingertips against
blood-stained stones: monk's blood,
the children said, slain by Cromwell.
Spillage the color of nail-rust.

Forty years and I hear from my cottage
the parish priest on a loudspeaker,
his parishioners gathered close.
The country air passing over fields
warps the words out of their contours.
Continuity, especially from sad times,
requires open air and amplification.
Thinking how the human voice
managed once, without clang
and cloud echo.

That evening I go among the graves and,
bending to straighten a pot, am surprised
by nettles. She who lies there takes means
beyond the grave, to shrive me. So many ways
to touch beyond words.

When, next day, harsh words lash
from a visitor, I feel through sting
to that earlier tang of unlikely meeting
in the abbey yard, flesh
spoken to as flesh.

Midnight Lantern

It takes so little
of this slower, this handheld,
not-enough light
to relieve its forest. It cannot
dispel but shakes a chasm of passage
into night.

In the turf-warmed kitchen,
card playing for halfpennies.
The children are cheating
and their elders let them, prolonging
the delicious moment
they gleefully restore order, "put
manners on them."

Tom Conlon, dreading
ghosts, yet needing to go home.
Mrs. Killoren lights the midnight lantern,
sees her neighbor to the foot
of Laherdan Lane, then turns back alone,
walking as a lantern does, giving onto
what rises up.

Eighty years since, the deck trimmed
to its box. Other card players
stand quietly on the stoop
for good-byes along the lake road, hearing together
swans ruffle the darkness
in one burst of unsettled agreement.

I walk myself across death and time
toward the lake, thinking in wing-rush: Mrs. Killoren
must hear them, must be putting the ghosts
back to dark along her hedges,
as I am opening
my hedge-heart by swan-cry to the lake.

We brave into ourselves each time
we put on our lantern-light
and step out—as a gleam steps
out its overlapping forms
to lift a path from its nest of darkness.

And now I think Mrs. Killoren must be safely home.

NOTES

Togetsu Bridge: "Moon Crossing Bridge" is a translation from the Chinese characters for the Togetsu Bridge, which spans the river Oi near Kyōto in the Arashiyama area, known for the many important literary works that celebrate its beauty. In the days of the aristocracy there was a fanciful custom called *Ogi-nagashi* of floating fans down the river from boats.

The mountain area on the Sagano side of the bridge is also known for its many temples and as a retreat area for those wishing to take up lives of solitude. As I walked across the Togetsu Bridge in late November 1990 with two Japanese friends, it occurred to me that I had literally just walked across the title of my book.

The name of the bridge is said to be an allusion to the moon crossing the night sky.

The epigraph for *Moon Crossing Bridge* is from *Poems of Paul Celan,* translated by Michael Hamburger.

"Cherry Blossoms"
Sotoba: A long, narrow wooden tablet set up near a grave, inscribed with a sentence from the Buddhist sacred books, and the name of the deceased; supposed to facilitate the entrance of the soul into paradise.

"Un Extraño"
In the lexicon of bullfighting, *un extraño* is the sudden deadly lunge a bull can make. In common usage, *extraño* is an adjective meaning strange or odd or foreign. An *adorno* is the kiss or

touch a matador sometimes gives the bull as a sign of respect before the kill. *El novillito:* little black bull.

"Kisses from the Inside"
The woods of Soto are near where Federico García Lorca was raised in Andalusia.

"Near, As All That Is Lost"
The epigraph is by Francis Travis, spoken while instructing the volunteer orchestra in Tokyo, Japan.
Morenito: little dark one.

"Sah Sin"
Sah Sin is the Nootka word for hummingbird.

Acknowledgments

Grateful acknowledgments are made to the following publications where some of the new poems in the *Signature* section have appeared:

Cerise Press: "Barrie Cooke Painting" and "Between the Voice and the Feather"

The Los Angeles Review: "Maurice's Foal"

The New Yorker: "The Tallest Men in Europe"

The Salt River Review: "Sruthlinn Spring"

The Stinging Fly (Dublin): "Perished" and "Red Perch"

"Brushing Fate," "Lie Down with the Lamb," and "Irish Weather" first appeared in *Dear Ghosts,* published by Graywolf Press in 2006.

I would like to offer deep gratitude to Greg Simon and Alice Derry for their devotion to poetry, and in particular their invaluable work on this volume.

The support of the painter and storyteller Josie Gray has been ongoing for the past nineteen years. His paintings and sense of humor are sustaining, and our life together at Abbey Cottage on Lough Arrow made it the site of many recent poems.

I'd like to give thanks for both my American and Irish families, particularly my sister, Stevie, and her poet son Caleb Barber, whose suggestions were a guide. Sheila Gray, her brother Edmund, his wife Norma, and their daughter Karen, have enriched my continuing Irish life at Ballindoon. Gemma, Siobahn, Mirium, and Eileen Frazer keep such welcome for me that I treasure my returns. The long friendship of Eileen and Maurice McDonagh goes back to my first readings of poems in their parlor during the Vietnam War. I was their guest while

I was writing *Under Stars,* and their daughter Yvonne is a strong figure in several of my poems.

Dorothy and Dick Catlett have been my Port Angeles stalwarts—Dorothy contributing more than could really be voiced in her constant championing of my work and the deep involvement we shared in it during the nine years she was my private secretary.

Meals with Alice Derry and Bruce Murdock were lovely islands in the solitary domestic zone I inhabit during the writing.

Bill Stull and Maureen Carroll gave excellent scholarship to Raymond Carver's *Collected Stories.* They also helped me fulfill my long-held wish to bring out *Beginners* alongside Ray's other books, freeing me to return to my own writing.

Alfredo Arreguin, Susan Lytle, Sean McSweeny, Nick Miller, and Barrie Cooke are among the many painters who have influenced me, and warmed my spirit with friendship and welcome. Sheila McSweeny's photographs of the bogs of North Sligo, and of sea/skyscapes, have entered my deepest eye. Novelist and poet Dermot Healey and his wife Helen have sweetly made lively my time in county Sligo. The novelist and poet Leland Bardwell helped launch *Dear Ghosts,* in Ireland. And, as a great storyteller, she helped me comprehend the struggle of Irish women in literature.

Belfast poet and novelist Ciaran Carson has been an inspiration for thirty-five years. Mebdh McGuckian, also a Belfast poet, brought early to my consciousness the way an uncanny emotional and intellectual ambush could outleap what one thought poetry could be, to open things up bravely, entirely.

My early times in Belfast in the company of Michael Longley, Edna Longley, and Paul Muldoon nurtured me in ways I still carry. Recent appearances at No Alibis Bookstore in Belfast, with Martin Donnelly as a guest of David Torrans, have helped hold my presence in this unforgettable city of my youth.

I'm always in mind of Raymond Carver—*Nothing can stop our tenderness.*

TESS GALLAGHER is the author of eight volumes of poetry, including *Dear Ghosts, Moon Crossing Bridge,* and *Amplitude.* She is also the author of four collections of short fiction, including *The Man from Kinvara: Selected Stories* and *Barnacle Soup: Stories from the West of Ireland,* a collaboration with the Irish storyteller Josie Gray. She has also published two works of nonfiction, *Soul Barnacles: Ten More Years with Ray* and *A Concert of Tenses: Essays on Poetry.* With Adam J. Sorkin and Liliana Ursu, Gallagher has translated two books of poetry by Ursu, *A Path to the Sea* and *The Sky behind the Forest.* She initiated the publication of Raymond Carver's *Beginners* in the Library of America's complete collection of his stories. She spends time in a cottage on Lough Arrow in Co. Sligo in the West of Ireland, where many of her new poems are set, and also lives and writes in her hometown of Port Angeles, Washington.

Composition by BookMobile Design and Publishing Services, Minneapolis, Minnesota. Manufactured by Friesens on acid-free 100 percent postconsumer wastepaper.

DATE DUE

DEC 1 6 2011		
JAN 2 4 2012		
SEP - 7 2017		
DEC 2 8 2020		